This book is an oasis of understand the what, when, and how of using spiritual gifts. Doris did an awesome job highlighting the perils of not using the tools God has made available to His people. She gracefully illustrates the balance between freedom to flow in spiritual gifts, as well as the necessary accountability and wisdom needed to be effective for God's kingdom. I believe many will come away after reading this book with a sense of urgency and encouragement to move forward in all God has graced them to be and do. I look forward to hearing the testimonies that will be a result of this book. It is well worth the investment!

—PROPHET DARRYL DAVIS
SYCHAR MINISTRIES

Gifts of Grace: Seven Keys to Discovering Your Hidden Potential by Doris E. Golder is both refreshing and educational for the Christian community today. Her God-given wisdom and anointing are a blessing for all. This book is full of wisdom and help for the Christian who has received hurts and wounds from church leaders in his/her own congregation. May this book bless Christian leaders and layman alike.

—VEOLA DUNN, LSW
ASSOCIATE PASTOR, HOUSE OF PRAYER CHURCH, #4
FT. MYERS, FL

Doris Golder is a longtime friend of mine. I call her my big sis. We have worked together in ministry for many years. She is a person who does not let distractions stop her from moving forward. She puts her whole heart into everything she does with perfection and impressive quality. Doris does not do anything without prayer and the wisdom of God. It is God who has inspired her to write this book, and as you read, you will see the heart of God on every page.

Doris has the heart to reach out to people from all walks of life, and she absolutely adores children. Some of her workshops included gathering back-to-school supplies for children and workshops for teens and adults. Doris always puts others before herself, and I have learned so much from her.

Doris is a strong, intelligent, and sincere woman of God. She will encourage you until you feel like you can conquer anything. She will labor with you in prayer until you reach a level of confidence that you did not know you had.

To all who read this book, you will be inspired, encouraged, and empowered to handle any situations, conquer all your fears, and be victorious in everything you set your mind to do.

God bless you, Doris. My prayers are with you.

—ANNA HOLCOMB
PROPHETIC TEACHER,
CHANGING LIVES THROUGH PRAYER

Doris E. Golder's emphasis on the fact that there is GREATNESS on the inside of each individual, cuts down the spirit of fear that plagues so many preventing them from moving forward and taking risks. "Risk Takers", work hand in hand with GOD to see the full manifestation of what HE has promised. Powerful read for those who are really ready to embrace what they have been called to do.

—APOSTLE BARBARA J. MCCLAIN
FOUNDER, BARBARA MCCLAIN MINISTRIES,
KINGDOM INTERNATIONAL INSTITUTE

Doris Golder is a sound prophetic teacher who walks diligently in her call to prepare the body of Christ for this End-Time revival. *Gifts of Grace* will equip you to use your God-given gifts to better impact your sphere of influence.

—EVANGELIST PATTY MOORE, LCSW
AUTHOR AND RADIO HOST, TRUMPETS OF TRUTH

I am extremely excited to see the vision of the visionary come forth. I sincerely believe this is a very timely message. A message that will not only help others discover their hidden potential but will also provoke and activate them to pursue their dreams and visions.

—Apostle George Pearson III
Kingdom Now Training Center

Minister Doris Golder, a woman of God and standard-bearer of God's Word, realizes that His Word has given her direction and ordered her steps in the process of her kingdom journey. Reader, please allow the biblical principles and concepts that she shares in her book *Gifts of Grace: Seven Keys to Discovering Your Hidden Potential,* to permeate your soul and ignite your spirit as your purpose and potentials are revealed by the Holy Spirit.

—VernElla Smith
Prophetic minister, Created to Serve Ministry
Christian International Family Worship Center
Versailles, IN

In this book, Doris expresses her heart for those who desire to discover and flow in their God-given gifts. She uses a very practical and easy-to-understand approach to the seven keys that aid in the discovery of one's potential. You are drawn into the narrative with stories and examples that emphasize each key. This book is a must read not only for those who are in the process of discovering their gifts, but also for those who desire to expand to greater exercise of their hidden potential.

—Pamela Thomas
Christ for the World Ministries, Inc.

GIFTS *of* GRACE

SEVEN KEYS TO DISCOVERING YOUR HIDDEN POTENTIAL

DORIS E. GOLDER

GIFTS OF GRACE: SEVEN KEYS TO DISCOVERING YOUR HIDDEN POTENTIAL
by Doris E. Golder
Published by D'Vine Strategies LLC
PO Box 20052
Indianapolis, IN 46220
doris@dvinestrategies.com

Editor: Jevon Bolden and Embolden Media Group
Author photo by: Phylisia Donaldson

Visit the author's website at www.dvinestrategies.com.

International Standard Book Number: 978-1-7338534-0-8
E-book ISBN: 978-1-7338534-1-5

20 21 22 23 24 — 987654321
Printed in the United States of America

To God alone be the glory for all the things He has done. He is the head of my life and my source of joy. During my short time on earth, He has taken me to places in Him that I never thought I would go, and I continue to look for more. The best is yet to come. Without Him, the concepts in this book would not have been conceived and now birthed to bless others.

I dedicate this book to my husband, Halden, who has been with me through the journey of risk and stages of spiritual growth. Thank you and much love for your patience and support during the process.

To my son, Nicolas, who is the light of my life, whom God allowed me to birth at a time in my life when selfishness would have tainted my view of reality, and who let me enter his world to experience his challenges as an adolescent, teen, and adult: I see your success. Dad and I are so proud of you and what you have become. Continue to maximize your talents to reach your potential. Explore and embrace all the Master has for you.

To my parents, Eddie and Brooksie Morgan (now deceased), who embraced their gift of grace and fulfilled their purpose with passion as pastors of a multicultural church: "You helped me become the woman I am today." You saw the gifts in me at an early age and allowed me the wings to fly.

Thanks to Charles and Eddie, my brothers: You are my biggest encouragers.

To my sister, Cora, now deceased: Your words are still with me today, "It will happen according to God's time."

To my beautiful stepdaughter, Trina. You are destined for greatness. The talents you possess can open doors of unlimited possibilities. Take the seven keys with you as you set out to discover your hidden potential. Receive and fulfill all the great things the Master has for you.

To all my former high school students, who were challenged with many obstacles yet persevered with courage and were inspired to reach the goal of graduation: Some said you would never make it, but you did. You won! Thank you for the honor of letting me walk alongside you and be part of your journey and success. Dreams are possible with desire and hard work.

To my spiritual sons and daughters in the faith, near and far, who received the spiritual and life nuggets that I imparted along the way: Your fruits have ripened to see the gifts of grace flourish through your established ministries and leadership roles. This is a true testament of the Master's faithfulness.

To my former spiritual father and pastor, Bishop Morris E. Golder, who is now gone on to be with the Lord: You will never know the impact your death had in transitioning me out of my comfort zone and helping me to take the risk to move forward and begin to fulfill my destiny.

CONTENTS

Acknowledgments xv

Introduction xvii

PART I
LAYING THE FOUNDATION

1 — The Secret 1

Embrace the Shift. 3

The Seed. 5

Ultimate Son Light. 5

Questions for Personal and Group Reflection. 6

Meditation for Transformation 7

Your Grace in Action. 7

Prayer of Partnership. 8

2 — Discovering Your Gifts of Grace. 9

Desperate for More 10

Opportunity to Serve. 14

The Power of the Body 15

We Are One. 16

Anointed with One or More Gifts. 16

Strengthen Others with Your Gift. 17

Two Building Blocks 17

Four Steps to Walk in Your Gifts 18

Questions for Personal and Group Reflection. 19

Meditation for Transformation 19

Your Grace in Action 20

Prayer of Partnership 20

**3 — Establishing and Activating
   Your Gifts of Grace** **21**

A Brief Description of Spiritual Gifts 22

Gifts of Grace and the Next Generation 30

"My Gift" 30

Activation Is the Password 34

Questions for Personal and Group Reflection 35

Meditation for Transformation 35

Your Grace in Action 35

Prayer of Partnership 35

4 — Overcoming the Fear of Risk **36**

Combat the Fear 37

There Is Greatness Inside You 39

1. The Man Who Would Be a Deliverer 40

2. The Young Man Who Refused to Let
   His Destiny Be Threatened 41

3. The Woman Who Refused to Be Status Quo 42

Overcome the Fear of Risk 43

The Supreme Risk-Taker 45

Questions for Personal and Group Reflection 46

Meditation for Transformation 46

Your Grace in Action 47

Prayer of Partnership 47

5 — Hidden in the House **48**

Church as Home and Family 48

The Pastor Sets the Atmosphere 49

Becoming an Effective Team Member 50

Planted for a Season. 51

How Did I Get Here?. 53

The Wounded Member. 54

Where Do I Fit? 55

Timing Is Everything. 57

Questions for Personal and Group Reflection. 59

Meditation for Transformation 59

Your Grace in Action. 59

Prayer of Partnership. 60

**6 — Your Anointing Is Too Costly
for You to Remain Quiet** **61**

The Essence of His Fragrance—the Anointing. 62

What Is the Anointing?. 62

The Anointing Creates Change 64

The Anointing Is Costly 64

The Anointing Is Not Quiet. 65

The Anointing Changed My Life. 66

For Such a Time as This 68

Your Assignment Will Require the Anointing 70

Questions for Personal and Group Reflection. 70

Meditation for Transformation 71

Your Grace in Action. 71

Prayer of Partnership. 71

7 — Your Seat of Destiny **72**

The Purpose of Your Seat of Destiny 73

The Gate of Access. 74

Marketplace Experience 75

The Master's Signature Is on Your Paperwork 77

Prepare to Shift. 78

Time for the Unveiling 82

My Mission or Ministry Assignment 84

Questions for Personal or Group Reflection 85

Meditation for Transformation 85

Your Grace in Action. 86

Prayer of Partnership. 86

PART II
BUILDING YOUR SPIRITUAL TOOLBOX

8 — The Key of Wisdom **90**

The Word of God Is Wisdom. 92

The Value and Reward of Wisdom 92

Questions for Personal and Group Reflection. 93

Meditation for Transformation 94

Your Grace in Action. 94

Prayer of Partnership. 94

9 — The Key of Prayer **95**

Jeremiah, Prayed to Pass His
Assignment to Another. 95

Hannah—the Woman Who Was Childless. 96

Daniel—the Youth Who Prayed 97

Means of Communication 99

Purposes and Principles for Prayer. 100

Questions for Personal and Group Reflection. 104

Meditation for Transformation 104

Your Grace in Action. 105

Prayer of Partnership. 105

10 — The Key of Faith 106

Faith—the Five-Letter Word 107

Your Favorite Chair 107

Opponents of Faith 108

Disbelief and Fear 108

Our Model of Faith 109

Questions for Personal and Group Reflection. 110

Meditation for Transformation 110

Your Grace in Action. 111

Prayer of Partnership. 111

11 — The Key of God's Word—Your Compass 112

A Compass. 113

The Company Handbook 113

Questions for Personal and Group Reflection. 115

Meditation for Transformation 115

Your Grace in Action. 115

Prayer of Partnership. 116

12 — The Key of Accountability 117

The Purpose of Accountability 117

Is Trust a Lost Trait Today? 118

Let This Cup Pass 119

The Role of a Mentor. 120

Qualities of a Mentor. 123

Obedience Pleases the Heart of God 124

Questions for Personal and Group Reflection. 125

Meditation for Transformation 125

Your Grace in Action. 126

Prayer of Partnership. 126

13 — The Key of Preparation. **127**

   Awakening. 127

   You Can Begin Again 129

   Questions for Personal and Group Reflection. 131

   Meditation for Transformation 132

   Your Grace in Action. 132

   Prayer of Partnership. 134

14 — The Key of Timing. **135**

   Chronos Time. 136

   Kairos Time. 136

   A *Kairos* Moment. 137

   Be a Good Steward of Time 138

   Redeem the Time. 140

   The Secret Is Out 141

   Question for Personal and Group Reflection 141

   Meditation for Transformation 142

   Your Grace in Action. 142

   Prayer of Repentance and Restoration 142

The Charge 144

Suggested Resources 145

Notes 146

About the Author. 153

Contact Information 153

ACKNOWLEDGMENTS

THERE ARE SO many to whom I would like to express my gratitude:

My mentors—Deborah, Beulah, and Vee—who were relentless in their encouragement to write this book to bless and motivate others to change their position and fulfill their purpose.

My team of intercessors—Adrienne, Diane, Lady Barbara, Lady Anngel, Mary, Chonita, Carlisa and Pastor/Dr. Carol Ann Abbett, who bombarded the heavens for the finishing anointing to cover me so I would complete the book.

Roger and Tina Brett, who supported me unselfishly with their resources and friendship.

My editor, Jevon Bolden, a gifted young woman, who helped me to shape this book to share or convey the words in my heart to you the reader—thank you, Jevon.

INTRODUCTION

FROM THE BEGINNING of time, we have been on the Master's mind. In fact, when He created Adam and Eve, He placed within them talents and abilities that centered on organization and helps. What we'll later discover are gifts of grace, so they could take care of the Garden of Eden and, together, reach their potential. God made Adam to be a provider and protector for Eve, and Eve to be a helpmeet to Adam so he would not be alone.

The Master has given potential and purpose to everyone and everything He created. The animals have the potential to reproduce after their own kind. The flowers have the ability to give beauty and fragrance to the environment. In some instances and cultures, they provide flavor and fragrance to foods. The sun has the ability to create light for our day, and the moon and stars are a source of light at night.

Potential is defined as "capable of being or becoming."[1] God has created every human being with the capacity to be or become something more, and He is calling each of us to fulfill our purpose.

As you walk this journey through the next fourteen chapters, you will be strengthened and empowered to explore and fulfill your God-given assignment and destiny. You will be compelled to embrace and use the potential God has placed in you from the foundations of the earth.

Because the Master is a Spirit, He has created us to be His hands, feet, and voice. His purpose for us is to edify (build up), comfort (extend hope), and encourage (support) not only those in the body of Christ but also those in the marketplace.

As you begin to engage the principles in this book, you will notice that I use the term *gifts of grace* to refer to what are commonly called the spiritual gifts. I chose this expression to illustrate that you are God's best-kept secret, with hidden potential ready to be discovered to accomplish in Him all that He has designed you for. The word *grace*, as you may know, is connected with supernatural spiritual power to do the things God has commissioned us to do. Our gifts are divine graces placed upon us to do extraordinary things.

To help you know the graces that are available to you, I will begin my focus on the varied gifts of grace noted in specific scriptures in the New Testament. Of these gifts, some are revelation gifts (in other words, they reveal something), some are utterance gifts (they cause you to say something), and some are power gifts (they cause you to do something). God has given each of us at least one of these gifts. You will learn how to discover your gifts of grace, their purpose, and why they are vital to the body of Christ and the marketplace.

Throughout my life, I always searched to discover my gifts and talents. I knew there was more. I had this strong sense that whatever we are called forth to do, we can and we must do it! You may be feeling this sense of urgency as well. That is why at the end of each chapter, I have included four elements or components to assist you to study and pursue more knowledge about your gift or gifts of grace:

1. Questions for personal and group reflections—During your personal or private devotion, read each question and write the answer or thought that best reflects what you feel. You may also choose to coordinate a Bible study group and invite others to share their gifts.

2. Meditation for transformation—A thought or belief to empower you as you make a shift.

3. Your grace in action—The purpose of the activity is to dig deeper, explore, and put in practice your feelings or thoughts with a positive hands-on, action-oriented application.

4. Prayer of partnership—What privilege and honor it is to invite God, our heavenly Father, to be our Partner in prayer on this journey He has developed for us. With this element, we will stand in faith and agreement on His promises that He will empower us to be all that He created us to be. When we fall short or become discouraged, His Word records the Lord boldly declaring to us, "'I will never leave you nor forsake you.' So we may boldly say: 'The Lord is my helper; I will not fear. What can man do to me?'" (Heb. 13:5–6).

It is my hope that these four elements will drive the points in each chapter deeper into your heart and spirit, helping you to become confident and determined to fulfill the call God has on your life.

I am also going to use the lives of several biblical characters and one woman in history to show you how to overcome the fear of risk and begin to step out. These people took risks to fulfill their assignments and changed the course of their lives forever.

You will come to understand that you can no longer be hidden in your sanctuary or place of worship because your anointing is too costly for you to be quiet. It's time to be released and walk in the power of God.

Did you know that you have a seat of authority? Once you discover and explore your gift, it's time for you to take authority and begin to walk with purpose to fulfill your assignment.

After we have discovered our gifts of grace, I will share seven keys that will help prepare you to move forward in your gifts and fulfill God's purpose for your life. Or perhaps you feel as if your season or appointed time to accomplish your assignment has passed, keep reading and do not despair. In the second half of the book, I will also share the two kinds of time that govern our lives and how you can redeem the time. It's never too late.

I invite you to turn the page to explore, embrace, shift, and allow God to take you places in Him that you have never been but have long desired to go.

PART I

LAYING THE FOUNDATION

Before we explore the seven keys for using your spiritual gifts to fulfill your purpose in the earth, I want to lay a foundation that will prepare your heart to receive the keys. Part 1 of this book will help open your eyes to what God has placed within you and how He wants to use it to build His kingdom and demonstrate His love and power in the earth. The possibilities of what you can achieve in God are endless, and achieving them begins by recognizing the gifts and talents God has given you and learning to use them for His glory. God has a great plan for you, and only you can fulfill it.

In the following chapters, I will show you how to discover and activate your gift and overcome your fears of stepping out into the unknown. Then we will discuss how to deal with seasons when you are "hidden in the house" before being released into your seat of destiny.

What God has placed within you is too valuable for you to keep it to yourself. The world needs your gift. So, let's learn how to discover your assignment and begin to walk in it!

Chapter One

THE SECRET

C<small>AN YOU KEEP</small> a secret? When I discovered all God had for me as His child, I realized what I could accomplish. When I realized how powerful I can be in God and the plans He has for me, all the limitations I thought existed disappeared. There are no limits in Him. The sooner you realize that, the sooner you will begin to fulfill your destiny in the earth.

Consider this: There is no one who has fingerprints, footprints, imagination, thoughts, or a smile like yours. You were born with God-given, natural talents passed down from your parents or ancestors through DNA. Parents have an innate ability to discern—from infancy through the teen years—the various talents their child possesses.

Talents have to do with natural abilities. They are significant in the physical, social, and emotional growth of a child to guide and motivate them in discovering who they are, what abilities they were born with, how those abilities will shape their lives, and the roles those abilities will enhance as they develop into healthy individuals. Talents play a major role in our life. When cultivated with care, they build our confidence and self-esteem and lead us to set life goals in regards to education, careers, and so on.

Psychologist Erik Erickson says there are eight stages of psychosocial development an individual will experience.[1] His stage five—identity vs. role confusion—is the one I want to focus on for our discussion here, which is the "adolescent

1

period from twelve to eighteen years." This may be the most challenging stage of life to navigate. It is a time when we are searching "for a sense of self and personal identity, through an intense exploration of personal values, beliefs, and goals."[2]

Do you remember your adolescent years? Do you remember how you explored various roles to see where and how you fit in? Maybe you chose the wrong friends. Maybe you felt isolated. Those experiences were the awakening that led you to believe that things had to be better when you reached adulthood.

The process of discovering who we are may take a lifetime. Most likely, your parents can vividly remember those years and may not want to revisit or be reminded of them. Erickson concludes, "Failure to successfully complete a stage can result in a reduced ability to complete further stages and therefore an unhealthier personality and sense of self."[3] In other words, it is important to go through each phase of life, even with its ups and downs, triumphs and difficulties, if we are to grow into balanced and healthy individuals. Consequently, we must have proper emotional, physical, and spiritual nourishment to become strong and vibrant to reach our full potential that is expressed through our talents and gifting.

Maybe you have a natural talent to sew, build things, or care for animals. As you grew through your adolescent years, the talent became stronger and you began to stretch further. You designed your own clothes. You helped your parents build a picnic table, or you volunteered at an animal shelter.

You were uniquely designed and gifted by God to perform an assignment that only you can accomplish. At an early age, you may not have known about the natural talents that sat dormant within you, waiting to be ignited. As a result, you may have been reluctant to acknowledge what you sensed, even fearful to step out and allow that seed to grow and fulfill the purpose God designed for you. This is why I have written this book: so we can explore together your greatness and learn how to develop the potential within you.

EMBRACE THE SHIFT

I grew up in a small Midwest community where resilient faith, basketball, and the automobile manufacturing industry were our heartbeat. Two generations of my family members were assembly line workers, and one generation was skilled as trade professionals committed to excellence in their jobs at the automobile plant. They were content and proud to earn salaries that provided a good living for their middle-class families.

At the end of the day, with school work and chores completed, we gathered around the dining room table to break bread and share the current community news. As always, our conversation would end on the undefeated wins of our hometown basketball team, the Indians, against whatever rivals dared to step on the court and challenge them.

Our faith in God was the common thread that bonded and kept our family together through tough times. We were confident that we could trust Him to take care of us no matter how challenging situations became.

Suddenly a major shift occurred that changed our lifestyle and the lives of other families in the community. One of the automobile companies was forced to cut cost whereby reducing the workforce through indefinite layoffs. Pink slips were distributed to alert approximately five hundred or more workers about this drastic change which could possibly lead to permanent job loss.

This unexpected shift left my family and others with a feeling of uncertainty about the future. Disappointment set in. Dreams and hopes of a brighter tomorrow began to diminish. Some workers were thrust into early retirement. Others relocated to various cities to search for job opportunities. In each scenario, their personal assignments had changed unexpectedly. The men, women, and their families were launched into a new season of their lives with the question, "How do we begin again?"

With determination, my parents moved forward, assessed their skill sets to see how they could survive the layoff, and establish sufficient earnings through self-employment. My mother was a licensed hairstylist and was excited to use her talent to bless others in the community. My father was gifted in carpentry and was known as the best peanut brittle candy maker in our town. Many people enjoyed the sweet delicacy during the Fall and Winter seasons.

During the unexpected transition from being employed to unemployed to self-employed, our family held on with strong faith and confessed daily God's promise, "We can do all things through Christ who strengthen us" (Phil. 4:13). Though we couldn't see all that God was doing, we trusted that He would be faithful to complete the work He had begun in us and that, even in the hard times, all things truly do work together for our good. Under few other circumstances would we have been given the blessed opportunity to witness God moving things around in our lives to bring us closer to walking in our unique purposes and destinies.

Our family's story may not be like yours, but you have one to tell and an incredible journey ahead of you. And I believe it is time to take a leap of faith and embrace the shift into the next chapter of your story by discovering and fulfilling your purpose.

Be confident. Time and preparation are two key components needed. God will give you the natural resources and spiritual tools you need to accomplish the plans He has for you and to be all He created you to be.

THE SEED

Our natural talents are like small seeds. They go through many stages of growth. Left without proper stimulation or continued use, they will not fully develop or help you reach your potential.

My husband is an avid gardener. He has a natural talent for gardening. Over the years, he has produced healthy vegetation for our family and others. He knows the process well. A plant begins as a small seed. Water and the right soil and climate are vital for the seed to produce a healthy plant. During the germination process, fertilizer is added to ensure the seeds become strong.

My husband is also aware that different plants need different elements to help them flourish. For example, he learned that tomato plants need lots of sunshine and the soil must not be extremely wet. Lettuce, on the other hand, is a cool-weather plant, and its soil must be well drained.

Every year he takes a risk to plant his seeds or flower bulbs not knowing how much they would produce. I once asked him, "What if you don't reap a harvest?" He said, "What if I never try? I know that I have the ability to make things grow!"

Sometimes we get stuck when thinking about how to grow our gifts because the process is challenging and we aren't sure of what the end product will be. Taking risks and getting out of comfort zones to discover what we are really made of can be scary, but it always yields a great harvest.

ULTIMATE SON LIGHT

Not only does my husband have the ability to make things grow, but he also knows the ultimate source through which things are created and developed. As it is with plants, to become all that you are meant to be, you must be connected to a power source—Jesus Christ. You may be reluctant to move because of the challenges that lie ahead. Still, I encourage you to take a leap of faith to connect with the Son light and let Him unlock the potential that is waiting to be released.

One of my gifts of grace, or spiritual gifts, is administration or leadership. We will discuss this gift more in chapter three, called "Establishing and Activating Your Gift of Grace." Two of my natural talents are organization and counseling. Both my natural talents and spiritual gifts help me assist youth and adults to develop their natural skills and discover and activate their spiritual gifts. I am also skilled at helping them find the resources they need to accomplish their assignment and purpose in the earth.

As I live under the light of the Son, I am watered by the Spirit of God and nourished by the love of God the Father, and the seeds that have been planted in me grow. The more I take risks and allow the seed within me to grow and multiply, the more I am able to be everything God created me to be.

God wants this same thing for you. You have spiritual gifts within you that are ready to be discovered. In the next chapter, we will examine what the Word of God says about spiritual gifts and His desire for you to learn, move, and be established in what He has placed inside of you.

QUESTIONS FOR PERSONAL
AND GROUP REFLECTION

1. What natural talents (such as singing, writing, or drawing) do you believe you were born with?

2. Have you nurtured these talents by learning how to do them better, or has life gotten in the way of your growth in these areas?

3. In what ways have you used these natural talents to assist or to bless others? What more do you see yourself doing as you get better at these talents?

MEDITATION FOR TRANSFORMATION

In Matthew 25:14–28, we find Jesus telling the Parable of the Talents. The illustration is about a landowner who went away on a journey and distributed to his three servants' goods or talents to use "according to their own ability" (v. 15). Upon returning from his trip and assessing the servants' work, the landowner found that two servants were successful and one was not.

1. What did the servant who was given the one talent do with his?

2. What do you think caused the man to bury or hide his talent rather than multiply it as the other two workers had?

3. Is there a talent or gift you have buried? What is it and why have you hidden it?

4. Would you like to find or rediscover it in order to bless others and bring glory to God?

YOUR GRACE IN ACTION

Write a brief thank-you letter to express your gratitude to a parent, guardian, teacher, or leader who has impacted your life, encouraged you to use your natural talents, and helped you develop into the person you are today. If you are under eighteen years old, please ask your parent or guardian to review the letter upon completion.

PRAYER OF PARTNERSHIP

Thank You, heavenly Father, for creating me after Your likeness. I am a mirror image of You, and Your greatness is reflected in me. As I set out on this journey to discover all You have created me to do, I know You will be my guide, and I will follow You. You have given me great potential, and I accept my responsibility to use my talents, gifts, and abilities to fulfill my purpose in the earth. I know that I have been blessed with the richness of Your gifts, and I will use them to bless others in the kingdom. In Jesus's name, I pray. Amen.

Chapter Two

DISCOVERING YOUR
GIFTS OF GRACE

Birthdays are a wonderful time to celebrate. Though birthdays have always been a delight in my family, we don't always come together each year to celebrate each member's birthday with the traditional cake and ice cream. Instead, we send congratulations with cards, telephone calls, and other expressions of love. We love to bless one another with gifts and recognition when we can.

God also desires to give His children beautiful gifts. One of them is the gift of salvation. This gift is priceless, life-changing, and irrevocable. He will never change His mind about His gift to you, nor can you return it to the store for a refund. Other gifts that God gives are the gifts of grace that bring His glory, blessing, and purpose into our lives. All of these gifts are so good and come from our Father who loves us.

When it comes to receiving gifts, have you ever witnessed a toddler trying to get something from their parent? It could be that they want attention, or maybe they're in the grocery store and some shiny toy has caught the child's eye and they want mommy or daddy to get it for them. They will pull on their parent's clothes, throw a tantrum, or find some way to let them know they need the parent to see about what they want or need. If they are successful, the parent will stoop down and incline their ear near their child's mouth to hear the urgent appeal.

Upon sensing our need, God pulls us to Him in a similar way. One day He tugs at our hearts and begins to draw us to Him, until we accept and commit our lives to Him and He becomes our Master. But He doesn't stop there. God loves us so much that He pours upon us gifts of grace that equip us to go forth to bless others. The urgency is now for you to step out, walk boldly without fear and embrace or accept all that God has created you to be.

I remember a time when I found myself in this similar place. I was crying out to God for more, yet I was afraid to reach out and grab it. There was such a struggle within me until I found the courage to step out and say yes to God. Because of my yes, I am now walking boldly in my destiny and helping others to find and fulfill theirs.

DESPERATE FOR MORE

For approximately seven years, I went on a quest to discover where I fit in the body of Christ and what my purpose is in the earth. I knew God desired and had more for me. Weary of mediocre worship and church services void of God's presence, I just did not know how else to tap into it. I had been a believer for years but never felt spiritually fulfilled.

As a young girl, I was taught to pray, to please God, and to read the scriptures daily. Part of my religious foundation was birthed in traditional standards. I was desperate to feel and experience the freedom Jesus promised to give when He said that He came that we may have life and life more abundantly (John 10:10).

There were times when I sensed I had failed God and a spirit of condemnation would hover over me like a dark cloud. I felt that God was not pleased with me. Around friends, family, and church members, I wore a mask to hide my true feelings. The mask gave me a sense of security that kept me from having to face the truth of the hurt and lack of fulfillment I experienced almost daily.

Oftentimes, I spent more time pleasing others who desired my time and talent to build works, than delighting in God who desired my heart and an intimate relationship with me. I was desperate to discover and identify God's call on my life so that I could be His true servant and accomplish all He created me to do. I was unaware of the unlimited possibilities I could achieve in God. I cried out to God for help. I longed for a divine makeover.

One day, as I read the Word of God, my eyes were drawn to Mark 9:29, which reads, "So He said to them, 'This kind can come out by nothing but prayer and fasting.'" I received my answer! God spoke to me through His Word. He directed me to set aside the month of January in 2011 for consecration. January was the first month of the year where many set personal and spiritual goals and reevaluate old priorities that do not align up with their vision for the New Year. The number twenty-one dropped in my spirit. I chose the first twenty-one days of January to fast.

God faithfully prepared the way for me to earnestly seek His face about what He wanted me to know concerning His plans for my life. At the time, I worked for a company and had a flexible schedule, so I was able to make the necessary adjustment to my work schedule. I shared with my husband the need to consecrate myself before God, and he supported me. I planned my meals ahead for my family so I would not be distracted with cooking each day. I prepared my secret place in a small area of my home away from the hustle and bustle of the family activities. I rose early in the morning to meet God. My fasting consisted of drinking water and eating only one meal each day, preferably dinner with my family.

On the first through fourth day, I sought, pursued, and

delighted in God with the tambourine and dance. I confessed who God's Word said I am in Him. I began with the scripture found in Romans 8:37: "I am more than a conqueror through Him that loves me." I knew that Jesus loved and wanted His best for me. Each day, I began to feel my spirit man get stronger. I prayed relentlessly seeking God to reveal to me His hidden treasures and the plan He had for my future. I asked Him to show me how to discover my gifts of grace and equip me to bless His people. When I was unable to pray alone or in secret, I prayed in my spirit while riding in the car, doing my low-impact exercises, or laundry.

On the fifth through ninth day, as I continued to press in through worship, the spirits of fear, pride, and unforgiveness began to diminish until they were gone. I began to praise God through meditating on the Psalms. Psalm 138:8 rose up in my spirit: "The Lord will perfect that which concerneth me," followed by Psalm 71:16, "I will go in the strength of the Lord." I heard new songs rise up from my belly that I never heard before. I began to leap and twirl in dance and shout in my prayer language.

On the tenth through fourteenth day, as I waited for my miraculous breakthrough, I realize that the Word of God was my nourishment. It was delectable, and it began to heal the dark places in my heart where guilt and condemnation were hidden. I begin to confess Romans 8:1, "There is therefore now no condemnation to those who are in Christ Jesus, who do not walk according to the flesh, but according to the spirit." I confessed this scripture three times until I felt the power of God rise up. The Master reassured me through His word that if I abide in Him and walk in the Spirit and not my own will, I will have no condemnation. Thank You, Father! I receive your promise.

On the fifteenth through nineteenth day, during my devotion time, I opened my Bible to read and my eyes were drawn again to a familiar passage of scripture found in Psalm

37:4–5, "Delight yourself also in the Lord, and He shall give you the desires of your heart. Commit your way to the Lord, trust also in Him, and He shall bring it to pass." It was as if a light bulb illuminated itself in my spirit.

The word *delight* is defined as "something that gives great pleasure."[1] Immediately, the cloak of armor I had worn for years fell off. Though I had read this scripture many times and quoted it throughout my life, I had never received the revelation I did that day.

God desires that I delight in Him and not in man or a religious agenda. He wants me to delight in Him, the true and living God who created me in "His image and according to His likeness…" (Gen. 1:26). The scripture in Psalms continues, "He shall give you the desires of your heart." As a result of finding enjoyment in God, your desires will be God's desires for you. King David, writer of this psalm, concluded by saying, "Commit your way…trust also in Him, and He shall bring it to pass." Praise God! As I make God first in my life, in His timing, His plans will be revealed and unfold for my life.

On the twentieth day of consecration, I saw an open heaven. It was as if God Himself came down to visit me and put His arms around me. He had released His ministering angels to wage war on my behalf. The spirit of oppression and any stronghold in my mind that had held me captive was broken and cast down. The Master handed me the prayer key to war on behalf of marriages and orphans. He told me how to do spiritual mapping in certain areas of my community to bring deliverance. I received a word of knowledge (or insight) from God on how to move forward strategically with this gift of grace to bless the body of Christ, to train and equip them in their various gifts.

The twenty-first and final day, God continued to speak to me through His Word and prayer. I meditated on His Word. I cried tears of joy and praise to God for the finishing anointing to complete my consecration and for manifesting Himself to me because I dared to step out to seek Him with all my "heart, with all my soul, with my entire mind and with all my strength..." (Mark 12:30).

Suddenly, a warm blanket of His love encircled me. It was as if the anointing oil had been poured on me and was running gently from the top of my head down to the bottom of my feet. He heard me, and my divine breakthrough and complete makeover were manifested as the tears of joy flowed and my body became alive with His presence. I felt whole, clean, and renewed.

You too can experience this level of breakthrough and revelation regarding how God has gifted and purposed you to live out His glory. You can live and fulfill your purpose as you pursue and delight in God. Do you hunger for more of God? Are you desperate to know that God has more for you than where you are now? Do not settle until you find a place in God that will fulfill the more that you were created for. If you know He is calling you to a time of consecration, worship, and fasting, obey Him. He will be faithful to not only hear your prayer, but to answer them as well.

OPPORTUNITY TO SERVE

The Gospels of Matthew, Mark, and Luke, and the Book of Acts have made a great impact on my life as a believer. Their scriptures are filled with the promises of God, and their records of the signs, wonders, and miracles Jesus performed help me to know God is still working in the earth today and desires to use us as part of this End-Time prophetic generation. It is exciting to learn that the Master has given us His seal of grace. Grace is not bought or earned. It is unmerited favor. God loved us so much that He sent the Holy Spirit with power that will transform us: "But you shall receive power when the Holy Spirit has come upon you; and you shall be witnesses to Me in Jerusalem, and in all Judea and Samaria, and to the end of the earth" (Acts 1:8).

It's amazing that the Master has endowed us with power to be eyewitnesses and share the good news of how we can be rescued through grace and become ambassadors for Him in our communities, cities, and the world. He gives us opportunities to use our gifts and talents for His service. There are particular assignments we have been called to do. Let's take a closer look at what those assignments are as we prepare to mobilize.

In his book *The Dynamics of Spiritual Gifts*, William McRae defines a spiritual gift or gift of grace as something that "is simply a divine endowment of a special ability for service upon a member of the body of Christ."[2]

The Greek word for "gift" is *charisma*. According to *Vines Expository Dictionary of New Testament Words*, one meaning of *charisma* is a "gift of grace, a gift involving grace, '*charis*' on part of God as the donor."[3]

The gifts given to us by the Holy Spirit empower us to serve God and others, and they enable us to fulfill our unique assignments in the kingdom. Every gift has different qualities and expressions. They can be displayed in as many ways as there are anointed people who use them. The Bible talks about this diversity of gifts as part of our supernatural power.

THE POWER OF THE BODY

The body of Christ is made up of the believers or members within the church or assembly. The Greek word *ecclesia* (ek-klay-see-ah), which comes from a root word that means "called out."[4] The members within the body of Christ must work together to advance the kingdom of God and His way of doing things so we can be equipped and effective to make a difference.

The church in Rome was reminded that there are many members within the body, and all do not function alike, yet they are one. Romans 12:4–5 says, "For as we have many members in one body, but all the members do not have the same function, so we, being many, are one body in Christ, and individually members of one another."

WE ARE ONE

Whether we are members of mega-churches or smaller works, we are all one body, but we do not all have the same functions, abilities, or gifts. The Master has made us for a specific purpose. We are created after His image and His likeness (Gen. 5:1), but He gifted us with varied functions.

To be an effective team in the kingdom, the members and leaders of the church must join together to create a force that the enemy cannot divide. To help the church at Ephesians understand this better, Paul compared the spiritual body of Christ to the human body. (See Ephesians 4.) Both must have nutrients, but in different ways. The human body needs proper nourishment to be strong, to function, and to effectively encourage continued growth. The spiritual body is effective when each part within it harmoniously performs its individual function with love.

When this happens, the body of Christ will experience an awakening, and many times, exponential growth will occur. (See Ephesians 4:16.) It is important for each member to discover their gift of grace and study what they are called to do as part of the whole body. More importantly, when believers walk confidently in their gifts, they encourage others in the faith.

ANOINTED WITH ONE OR MORE GIFTS

Every Spirit-filled believer of the New Testament church today is anointed with one or more gifts of grace. Spiritual gifts or gifts of grace are to be used to build up the body of Christ and to keep the church healthy.

The Corinthian church was noted for their carnality and the apostle Paul reminded them that he did not want them to be misinformed about the gifts of grace and how they were to be exercised. (See 1 Corinthians 12:1.) As modern-day believers, we too must be aware of the gifts and how to use them.

The Master gives to each believer a gift, determined by "one and the same [Holy] Spirit" as He chooses (1 Cor. 12:11). We cannot choose what gift we desire. God bestows generously to us of His good pleasure. As each of us has received a gift, we must "minister it to one another, as good stewards of the manifold grace of God" (1 Pet. 4:10).

STRENGTHEN OTHERS WITH YOUR GIFT

Faith is necessary as you walk in your gift. The Master desires that we walk with confidence and purpose, yet with a spirit of humility, as we build up the body of Christ. We should be sober or operating with sound judgment and a sound mind, not exalting ourselves in our abilities, because we each have a degree of faith that has been given to help strengthen others. (See Romans 12:3.)

TWO BUILDING BLOCKS

There are two essential building blocks believers must possess as they walk in their gifts. These two building blocks also strengthen the unity of the body. They are love and compassion. Both may require time to cultivate them fully, but each member needs them to fulfill their purpose within the body.

First, love is the greatest commandment. It is our honor to love the Father with our mind, will, and emotions because

He loved us first. Even greater is to love our neighbor as we love ourselves. (See Matthew 22:37–39.)

Second, compassion is about being able to deeply feel someone's pain. When we look outside our small world and view the needs of others, it will transform our minds and how we use and flow in our gifts of grace.

As we will soon discuss in chapter 3, the gift of mercy parallels compassion. This gift is also much-needed today in the body of Christ and the marketplace. The members who use this gift, for instance, will demonstrate compassion to the homeless in their cities by carrying blankets, nonperishable foods, socks, and other items to provide some small comfort.

FOUR STEPS TO WALK IN YOUR GIFTS[5]

The following steps will provide a safeguard as you move forward to discover and establish your gift.

1. Prayer is not an option. Ask God to reveal to you your gift and to confirm it with opportunities to exercise or practice it. Gifts can be misused if we do not exercise discipline. We do this with prayer. Use of proper protocol in handling your gift is critical. It is never our purpose to create confusion, division, or offense within the body and the kingdom of God. Our purpose is for God to receive the glory in all that we do and for His body to be edified.

2. Be sure to consult your pastor or leadership on their vision for use of gifts of grace in the church where you are a member. This will provide you with the proper spiritual protection and accountability.

3. Find a mentor or a member who is active in the gifts of grace who will walk alongside you and provide encouragement and guidance.

4. Be diligent in your Bible study to understand the purpose and nature of the gifts of grace and how they are used in the body of Christ.

This is an exciting time to be alive and to be part of what God is doing in the earth. Once you discover your gift (or gifts) of grace, be confident. God has anointed and distributed this gift to you, so go forth and bless the kingdom. But first, let's move on to chapter 3 to learn what the gifts are and how to discover which ones you've been given.

QUESTIONS FOR PERSONAL AND GROUP REFLECTION

1. Have you ever approached someone who appeared to be unlovable? What was your reaction? How did the individual who appeared unlovable respond to your approach? What led you to approach the person in the first place?

2. How does John 3:16 connect to love as the greatest commandment?

3. What was the Apostle Paul's response in his letter to those at Corinth about the spiritual gifts? (See 1 Corinthians 12:1–26.)

MEDITATION FOR TRANSFORMATION

If you have a friend who has lost their job and you learn they are without food, what is your first response to this situation?

a. Pray with your friend.

b. Tell someone about your friend's need.

    c. Call your church to see if assistance can be provided.

    d. Help your friend with the resources you have.

Through your response to the previous question, you may discover what one of your gifts might be. Remember your choice as we move on to Chapter 3 to see which gift aligns best with your answer.

YOUR GRACE IN ACTION

Find someone at your job or in your community this week and show them love by warmly greeting them or showing a special act of kindness.

PRAYER OF PARTNERSHIP

Thank You, heavenly Father, my Jehovah Jireh, for the gift of salvation. Thank You for Your spiritual gifts. I am grateful that there is one or more set aside especially for me, so I can be fitly joined together with the body of Christ. I will use my gift for Your glory and to honor, serve, and bless Your people. It will not be misused for self-gratification or vainglory, or to compete with others. With my gift, I can also be equipped to assist others in the marketplace to lift them up, encouraging and comforting them. Amen.

Chapter Three

ESTABLISHING AND ACTIVATING YOUR GIFTS OF GRACE

Mother Teresa, now known in the Catholic Church as Saint Teresa of Calcutta, was one of the most beloved individuals in the world. Around the world, she was well-known for her service to the impoverished and sick in the slums of India.

Her gift of mercy was recognized in 1979 when she was awarded the Nobel Peace Prize, which came with a monetary gift that she gave entirely to the poor.[1] Just imagine: if one woman's gift can change a world, how much more could we do as a body of Christ if we would use and confirm our gifts to demonstrate the kingdom of God in the earth?

Joy will arise not only when you identify your spiritual gift, but also when you learn how to establish it. As Alvin J. Vander Griend noted in his book *Discover Your Gifts and Learn How to Use Them*, this can be accomplished through "understanding, acceptance, involvement, prayer, getting involved in ministry, and evaluate the results."[2]

I am going to list and describe the gifts of grace that are outlined in Scripture within this chapter, but I also encourage you to attend a gift of grace or spiritual gifts workshop in your area. If you do not have access to a spiritual gifts class in your community, please consider an online search for the following training options: an online website class through YouTube, a webinar, audio podcasts,

CDs, or video teachings. Many local, national, and international ministries offer classes of various kinds on their websites. Another suggestion is to ask your leader if they would prayerfully consider developing a gift of grace class for new members to be trained and equipped in their gifts. The class will further assist you in identifying and confirming your gift. You will receive an in-depth understanding of your gift and a trained leader's guidance on how to properly activate it. You will also meet other believers who are committed to discovering their spiritual gifts and how they can be used in the local church.

If you have not identified your gifts of grace or spiritual gifts, I encourage you to order the questionnaire listed in the suggested resource section at the end of this book or a similar assessment tool that would have the gifts of grace listed. Remember, no one has every spiritual gift, but we each have at least one gift, which allows the body of Christ to function as one.

A BRIEF DESCRIPTION OF SPIRITUAL GIFTS

Approximately twenty spiritual gifts are noted in the New Testament. They can be found in Romans 12:6–8; 1 Corinthians 12:8–10, 28; and Ephesians 4:10–13. This list is not exhaustive, because I am including only the gifts found in these passages of Scripture.

> Having then gifts differing according to the grace that is given to us, let us use them: if prophecy, let us prophesy in proportion to our faith; or ministry, let us use it in our ministering; he who teaches, in teaching; he who exhorts, in exhortation; he who gives, with liberality; he who leads, with diligence; he who shows mercy, with cheerfulness.
>
> —ROMANS 12:6–8

For to one is given the word of wisdom through the Spirit, to another the word of knowledge through the same Spirit, to another faith by the same Spirit, to another gifts of healings by the same Spirit, to another the working of miracles, to another prophecy, to another discerning of spirits, to another different kinds of tongues, to another the interpretation of tongues....And God has appointed these in the church: first apostles, second prophets, third teachers, after that miracles, then gifts of healings, helps, administrations, varieties of tongues.
—1 CORINTHIANS 12:8–10, 28

He who descended is also the One who ascended far above all the heaven, that He might fill all things. And He Himself gave some to be apostles, some prophets, some evangelists, and some pastors and teachers, for the equipping of the saints for the work of ministry, for the edifying of the body of Christ, till we all come to the unity of the faith and of the knowledge of the Son of God.
—EPHESIANS 4:10–13

Utterance gifts

- Prophecy—the divine ability to give and receive an inspired utterance from the heart of God. It is one of the nine gifts of the Holy Spirit (Acts 15:32). Here's an example of the gift of prophecy in action. A prophecy can be given in various ways: one on one; a workshop group; a presbytery setting for ordination or when a believer is being commissioned into ministry. In addition, when a minister is preaching or teaching the congregation, they may sense the move of God and feel prompted by the Holy Spirit to also give a word of prophecy to an individual or a couple in the audience or the body of Christ.

- Different kinds of tongues—the divine ability to speak in a known language one has not learned, as happened in Acts 2:3–8. This is commonly called your prayer or heavenly language. God has promised this gift to every individual who desires it. It is free and received by faith.

  One may also have the divine ability to communicate a message in unknown tongues to the body of Christ. (See Mark 16:17.)

  Note: Please consult and follow the leadership of your pastor with regard to the use of this gift. Improper use or mishandling of the gift of tongues can lead to confusion and division.

- Interpretation of tongues—the divine ability a believer receives to also interpret a message given in tongues during the worship service. (See 1 Corinthians 12:10.) Again, please consult and follow the leadership of your pastor in regard to the use of this gift. Improper use or mishandling of this gift of tongues can lead to confusion and division.

Revelation gifts

- Word of wisdom—the divine ability that brings enlightenment, divine insight, and guidance to practically apply truth to various life situations. (See Acts 6:3; 1 Cor. 2:6–7.) Here's an example of the word of wisdom gift in action: Two individuals desiring to marry each other, both have spouses who are deceased and young-adult children still living at home. They will need guidance and counsel to assist them with effective ways to ensure the success of their marriage and blending their families. They need a word of wisdom.

- Word of knowledge—the divine ability to learn or seek truth by revelation, also works as a "knowing" given by the Holy Spirit. This ability can present itself through a situation, person(s), or thing. Here's an example of the word of knowledge in action: In Acts 5:1–10, husband and wife Ananias and Sapphira, lied to Apostle Peter when he asked them about the money from the land they sold. They lied to him and the Holy Spirit when they kept back part of the money.

- Discerning of spirits—the divine ability that allows a person to pierce the spirit realm and discern if an attitude, motive, or behavioral manifestation of a person or groups of people is of God; our enemy, Satan; or humans. Here's an example of the gift of discerning of spirits in action: Apostle Paul discerns a spirit of divination within a slave girl and "commanded it to come out in the name of Jesus" (Acts 16:16–18). In addition, read 1 John 4:1–6 to learn more about how to distinguish this kind of a spirit.

Power gifts

- Faith—the divine ability to have the confidence that God will answer whatever the need is. (See Matthew 8:5–10.) Here's an example of the faith gift in action: An individual's home may be in foreclosure and there is no personal money to pay the overdue balance. Instead of giving in to worry and trying to make things happen that could lead to less than prudent behavior, they commit themselves to prayer and believe God for a miracle. Then there's a knock on their door, and the individual at the door says, "The Lord laid you on my heart to bring this envelope over." The envelope contains the exact amount needed to bring the home mortgage current. Can God do this? Yes, He can!

- Healing—the divine ability to pray for the sick and see them recover supernaturally. (See Matthew 9:20–22.) Here's an example of the healing gift in action: A gentleman in his early fifties was diagnosed with a terminal illness, and the doctors had done all they could do. A week later, the condition worsened and the individual slipped into a coma. The family has been alerted that the end is near. A young man who was a former Sunday school member in the gentleman's class returned home on summer break to hear that his former teacher was extremely ill.

  When he went to visit his teacher in the hospital, he remembered what his teacher taught about healing: "If any of your family is sick, lay your hand on their hand and say boldly with confidence and belief, "Be healed in Jesus's name!" Feeling that this was the right moment and putting this teaching in action, the young man placed his hand on his teacher's hand and said, "Be healed in Jesus's name!" Then he left the room quickly.

  Two days passed, and the doctors checked the teacher's vital signs to see if there were any changes. Suddenly, the doctor noticed that his color had become brighter and the man had begun to move his fingers. Two weeks after that, the man was dismissed to go home with his family. Can God? God can! He is a healer.

- Miracles—the divine ability to bestow or facilitate supernatural interventions beyond the normal course. God still works miracles today. The gift of faith is a prerequisite in order for this gift to operate in a person's life. Healing is just one of the miracles a person with this gift can operate in. Here's an example of the healing gift in action: read the story of Naaman the leper, in 2 Kings 5:10–15. Through the prophet Elisha, God instructed Naaman to dip seven times in the Jordan River in order to be healed of leprosy. Naaman was obedient and received his healing.

Other gifts of grace found in 1 Corinthians 12 and Romans 12:4–8:

- Ministry—the divine ability to perfect and equip the saints for the work of the ministry. Here's an example of those who serve in the gift of ministry: Church leaders such as pastors, associate pastors, and those designated by the pastor or shepherd and others who are called by God. (Read Ephesians 4:11–12.)

- Exhortation—the divine ability given by the Holy Spirit to give encouragement or comfort through a scripture, counsel, or a spoken word. Here's an example of the gift of exhortation in action: A person goes to the home of one who is grieving after the loss of a family member or friend, and they deliver words that carry such a level of encouragement and comfort that the bereaved experiences unspeakable peace that allows great relief and assurance during their hard time. (Read Hebrews 10:24–25.)

- Giving—the divine ability to give generously to bless others in specific projects to advance the kingdom. Here's an example of the gift of giving in action: A servant who leads a nonprofit Christian organization and is seeking additional finances to complete the building of a new wing that will provide housing for the homeless and rehab for those who are bound through addictions. The person who sees this need and funds the effort would be one who walks in this gift of grace. (Read Romans 12:8.)

- Leadership—the divine ability to lead or direct people to set goals, focus, and fulfill their assignments within the body of Christ. Here's an example of those who serve under the gift of leadership: Pastors, associate pastors, and those who are designated by a pastor or shepherd and others who are called by God. (Read Hebrews 13:17.)

- Mercy—the divine ability to show compassion to those in need. Here's an example of someone who was a servant leader with the gift of mercy: Jesus, our Master, was the supreme example of mercy. (Read Luke 10:33–35 and Mark 1:41). Agencies such as local shelters, Salvation Army, Samaritan Purse, and others are just a few that demonstrate and extend mercy through kindness and support during some of life's most challenging situations.

- Helps—the divine ability to serve individuals and meet their needs in various ways. (Read Luke 8:3.) You may see the gift of helps in action in your community kitchen; the church pantry that provides food, clothes, and other supplies; and the church visitation and guest services departments that mail greeting cards to those who are sick and shut in and send out invitations to visit the church.

- Administration—the divine ability to organize and motivate people to carry out their assignments in the body of Christ. Here's an example of the individuals who assist with the gift of administration: The executive director, associate pastors, committee leaders, and more. (Read Titus 1:5.)

Fivefold ministry gifts

In Ephesians 4:10–13, Apostle Paul refers to the fivefold ministry gifts or offices as functions that Jesus set forth and placed within the body of Christ. Each carries the anointing and has been called to assist in their specific call or gifting for the body of Christ.

- Apostle—a person with the divine ability given by the Holy Spirit to establish or set forth foundational principles in our church culture today. These are those who we would call church planters or pioneers sent out in territories or regions to birth forth the gospel in areas that the gospel had not been preached nor heard. (Read 1 Corinthians 12:28.)

- Prophet—a person with the divine ability to hear and then speak the oracles and truths from God and deliver them to His people. An example of the prophetic gift in action: Read (Acts 21:10–14) the story of Prophet Agabus and Apostle Paul.

- Evangelist—the divine ability to win unbelievers to Christ by sharing the gospel of salvation. (Read 2 Timothy 4:5.) When a believer functions in the office of evangelist, we can expect to see revivals and camp meetings rise up in the foreign and domestic mission fields.

- Pastor—the divine ability to provide spiritual care for a body of believers. A pastor may also be called a shepherd because of the example Jesus set in John 10:1–18.

- Teacher—the divine ability to study and learn God's Word, to instruct, then impart or convey the information to others in such a way that will bring enlightenment and comprehension to their Christian walk. (Read Acts 18:24–28.) A pastor also operates in this gift. Here's an example of a gift of teaching: facilitate or lead a Sunday school class, Christian education department, a Bible study, or home cell group.

GIFTS OF GRACE AND THE NEXT GENERATION

As we move into the next season, it is vital that we begin to train and equip our youth, the next generation of warriors, for revival. This is an exciting time for them, but they must learn who they are in Christ and what God needs to do in order for them to be ready for battle.

We must prepare them and provide training in their Vacation Bible Schools, Christian education and leadership classes, youth retreats, and sports camps. They too can become powerful witnesses for the kingdom of God.

With the permission of the senior pastor, the youth leader can develop a gift of grace class to instruct the children and youth about the importance of learning their spiritual gifts. Upon completion of this training, each participant can shadow a seasoned (mature) adult or mentor who functions in a similar gift or call to their gift. Some of the gifts that the children or youth can learn to perform are junior ushers or doorkeepers, hospitality, media team or communication, leadership roles, and more.

I've provided the names of several books on gifts of grace for children and youth under "Suggested Resources" located at the end of this book.

"MY GIFT"

As I mentioned in the introduction, God has gifted me with the ability to help other people to discover their gifts. I have often led gifts of grace and spiritual gifts classes. Many of those who went through the class have sent me testimonies about how their lives changed when they learned more about who they were created to be in the kingdom of God. Since we have just discovered what the gifts of grace are, I would like to share some of the testimonies I have received. I pray that they encourage and bless you, and give you a picture of the confidence and joy that comes in knowing how you are specially created to be used by God.

> My natural talent is organization. I knew there was something within me that desired to be a person of excellence. I would seek jobs that were mediocre, until one day I realized that this was not me. I began to change my mind-set to seek careers that would show my strengths rather than weaknesses. One day I was invited to attend a spiritual gifts workshop to find out how I could be more effective in my church and bless others. Upon the completion of the class, it was evident that my gift was administration or leadership, which was also synonymous with my natural talent. Since this discovery, I have been extremely happy and fulfilled in my role as a leader. I have become the administrative assistant to the pastor of my church, and I organize and plan his calendar for church events.
>
> —SINCERELY, J

My natural talent is sewing and crafts. One of my spiritual gifts is the gift of helps. Helps is a gift that invests in the lives or ministries of others. It usually aids and enables individuals in increasing the effectiveness of their own spiritual gifts. Since I have identified my spiritual gift, I am more confident when moving in the spiritual dimension and when giving encouraging words to others.

Sometimes, I use my spiritual gift in the church to teach or exhort and encourage the body of Christ. I use my spiritual gift in the marketplace to pray for and bless others to be healed so they will know that God still is a healer today.

                                                        —SINCERELY, E

My natural talent is singing and reading. One of my dominant gifts of grace is the gift of exhortation. Discovering that God blessed me with the gift of exhortation has helped me to understand how I function in the body of Christ. In addition, I am learning that this gift can express itself in various ways, such as teaching and guidance. This is indeed an interesting gift that adapts to different expressions based upon what is needed at the time.

God has blessed me to use the gift of exhortation in my local church in praise service and choir and when encouraging individual church members.

In the workplace, colleagues and clients seek me out and begin conversations that lead them to ask me to share my thoughts on work or spiritual issues. There were times when I asked myself, "Why do they seek me to inquire about these hard questions?"

At the age of sixteen, individuals would welcome my thoughts on death, heaven, sickness, relationships, and more. Needless to say, I was challenged and sometimes perplexed at being stretched out of my comfort zone. However, I knew God was with me and was preparing me for something greater to encourage His people. As a result, God has now moved me from speaking on an individual level to a group level. Philippians 4:13 says, "I can do all things through Christ who strengthens me."

                                                        —SINCERELY, V

My natural talent is organization. One of my dominant gifts of grace is the gift of helps. I absolutely love helping others in any way I can. I'm always at the right place and at the right time to help someone. I don't mind being in the background because I'm there when and where I'm needed. I am currently serving on the administration and anniversary planning teams at my church.

—SINCERELY, C

My name is Nicole. I have been the owner of an accounting company, since September 2013. I'm a college graduate and earned a degree in business administration. I always dreamed of owning my own business but could never figure out exactly what I wanted to do. My background is in banking. I took a teller job when I graduated high school and worked there while finishing college. About three years later, I was offered an assistant manager position, which I gladly accepted and put my dream of owning a business on hold.

The position changed my lifestyle and spending habits. Everything was great until I had to get my taxes done. It was then I realized what people meant when they say, "More money, more problems."

I went to get my taxes done and was going to pay the service more to prepare my taxes than I was getting in a refund. Needless to say, I went home, looked up online tax sites, and did my own tax return. I thought it was easy and found it interesting because I like working with numbers. I started doing my friends' and family's taxes, which were basic tax returns. Then I wanted to learn how to do more complex returns, so I found tax classes and decided to go. After taking the classes, I was offered a job at a tax preparation company, working evenings and weekends. I still kept my job at the bank.

Working at the tax company allowed me to help people solve their problems and showed me the business side of taxes. I figured if they can make a successful business out of preparing taxes, so can I. I finally found something I enjoyed doing, so I decided to quit the tax preparation company and start working out of my home. I got new clients through social media and word of mouth, and I stayed in contact with some of my clients from my time at the tax company. I prepared over two hundred tax returns out of my home office and decided l wanted to take it to another level. I left my job at the bank and haven't looked back since.

Since writing this testimony, I took the spiritual gifts assessment to discover my gift of grace. Two of my dominant (stronger) gifts are faith and leadership. In addition, I have been blessed to purchase my own building.

—SINCERELY, NICOLE

ACTIVATION IS THE PASSWORD

Throughout the year, marathons are held for the avid walker, jogger, or runner. Those who commit to win will set a goal, prepare a rigorous training schedule, be diligent to practice each day, and even stretch beyond their capacity to win the event. By taking action toward their goals, they are, well, activating themselves—their potential, skills, and abilities— to see their goals accomplished.

The word *activation* means to mobilize. It is the key to unlocking the possibilities available for you to build up, comfort, and edify the body of Christ. Activation launches you into the full operation and flow of your gift so its ultimate benefit is that it blesses others.

It's humbling how God desires to use us to bless others with the gifts He gives us. Are you ready to see your gift change the course of someone's life? In the next chapter, we are going to talk about risk. You may have to take some risks as you begin to operate in your gift, but you are equipped through grace to handle any obstacle you may encounter.

QUESTIONS FOR PERSONAL
AND GROUP REFLECTION

1. Identify and list one of your gifts of grace, or spiritual gifts.

2. Share how you will use your spiritual gifts in your place of worship or the marketplace.

3. Does your church operate fully in the gifts of grace? If not, are you free to exercise your gifts of grace?

MEDITATION FOR TRANSFORMATION

The spiritual gift assessment or questionnaire is one spiritual tool to discover your gift of grace. I encourage you to find an opportunity to take this questionnaire and then write in your journal or notepad your experience. When you learned what your dominate gift of grace was, were you surprise, disappointed, amazed, or excited?

YOUR GRACE IN ACTION

This week find someone with whom to share your gifts of grace. To illustrate, if you have the gift of helps, ask a neighbor if you can assist them with lawn care or stock shelves at a local food pantry. After you have completed an activity that corresponds with your gift of grace, write down your thoughts about the experience. How did you feel operating in the gift God has given you?

PRAYER OF PARTNERSHIP

Thank You, Jesus, for my gift of grace. I commit to assist others in the body of Christ and the marketplace with this precious and priceless gift You have endowed me with. Amen.

Chapter Four

OVERCOMING
THE FEAR OF RISK

Risk is a part of life and so is change. Both are difficult to embrace but oftentimes are needed to be successful in life.

Each year, students prepare for high school graduation. They are excited to have completed four years of rigorous academic study. Many are eager to further their education at the college of their choice and pursue their career goals. Meanwhile, other students immediately will seek employment to become self-sufficient and independent of their parents.

In each situation, uncertainty about what the future will hold and the associated risks involved with achieving their goals could alter the student's plans. However, they must persist through the fear of risk if they are to see their goals come to fruition.

In his best-selling novel *Slam*, Walter Dean Myers vividly depicts a seventeen-year-old, a junior in high school, who excels on the basketball court with a goal of one day becoming an NBA star. But his poor academics may prevent him from reaching his goal.[1] Many power-packed scenes illustrate the key themes in this book, however, the times when the title character, Greg "Slam" Harris, takes a hard look at his life are the most poignant.

Upon coming face-to-face with decisions that will determine his future and being uncertain of whether his dream will come true, he concludes that life is not fair. Is life meant to be fair or is it made to be lived out with purpose to fulfill destiny, regardless of fairness? The small stuff such as struggles, distractions, heartache, and unfairness will birth a determination that will propel us into fulfilling our purpose. It is how we handle or interact daily with uncertainty that will determine our victory.

The young single parent who struggles with fear to meet the daily needs of their family is faced with the reality that, in order to survive, things cannot remain the same. They must take some form of risk to see a change in their circumstances. One example is to return back to school for additional education, which will increase their income and chances for a better job and lifestyle for their family. As a result, they will have to make changes to juggle the demands of a job, attend evening or online school, and care for their family in order to become a productive and self-sufficient citizen in today's society.

The elderly widow who survives on a meager budget fears that there will never be enough. She shutters at the thought of being alone but realizes that one day change will come. Oftentimes widows are seen as vulnerable and open prey to unscrupulous individuals who wish to cause them harm. Therefore, the widow is aware that changes may be needed and will reluctantly relocate to live with her family who will provide her with a safe place.

COMBAT THE FEAR

Risk is defined as "possibility of loss or injury."[2] I am not suggesting that you place yourself in a position that causes you physical or emotional harm. My goal is to share that, at times, we can be placed in helpless situations beyond our control from past hurts and wounds, yet you can be wholly set free to fulfill your destiny. There's also the simple fact that moving to higher level in life with God comes with a level of uncertainty, but He has given us power and a sound mind to take these challenges on with His wisdom and guidance.

If you think about it, individuals take risks each day in life to change their circumstances. Good choices to move forward and do better come with risk. In searching for a new job, one could risk being disappointed or rejected, but in the process, they build determination and confidence that, one day, the right job will come.

Increase in job title, income, or ministry platform may put some people at the risk of losing certain relationships. In these cases, friends and family are sometimes more comfortable with the person at one level and have a difficult time adjusting to the new level God brought them into.

Making a financial investment comes with a risk of loss, but there are also big opportunities for experiencing a higher standard of living.

Even with all these risks, God will carefully guide you through areas you've never seen or lived through before. With His wisdom as your close companion, I encourage you to push through the fear of taking certain healthy, wise, and calculated risks. You will surely come to a place of prosperity and success.

We are not born with an instruction manual for life, per se. Outside of the grace and wisdom that come from God, we were not prepared for the possible roadblocks that may occur on our spiritual journey. However, we do possess the most reliable handbook, the holy Bible, which gives us solutions to every problem we face. We can fight back against feelings of fear and doubt as we arm ourselves with the wisdom and truth of God's Word. Often this battle between fear and moving forward in the things God has designed for our abundant life is compared to combat. Combat may be defined as a "fight or struggle between two individuals or forces."[3] To resist fear will take courage. Keep your goal in mind. Have you identified what prevents you from moving forward? If so, are you ready to confront it? But first, pray for direction and that you will be led to the proper resources that will help you achieve success and move forward in victory.

Is there a fear you would like to overcome or conquer? Is it hindering you from stepping out and fulfilling a call on your life? If so, find a trusted friend who will walk with you and pray and stand in agreement with you until you receive your breakthrough.

If barriers such as age, lack of qualification, shyness, inability to speak, or poor socioeconomic status are in your way, this may be the time to release them as well so you can experience the freedom in God.

THERE IS GREATNESS INSIDE YOU

In the Book of Acts, prior to His ascension, Jesus met with His disciples (apostles) and gave them responsibilities to carry out. He encouraged them and gave them this promise: "You will receive power and ability when the Holy Spirit comes upon you; and you will be My witnesses [to tell people about Me] both in Jerusalem and in all Judea, and Samaria, and even to the ends of the earth" (Acts 1:8, AMP).

We are also reminded that we will perform "greater works" than the ones performed in Jesus's day (John 14:12). If you knew that the same power that was transferred from the Father to Jesus is also downloaded into you, what things would you take a risk to accomplish? It is an exciting revelation to know that when you step forward to carry out the assignment marked specifically for you, you cannot lose.

The word translated "power" in Acts 1:8 is the Greek word *dunamis*.[4] This is the term from which we get the word *dynamite*. In other words, we are equipped with an explosive spiritual power to do "great exploits" for the kingdom of God (Dan. 11:32). How reassuring it is to know that whatever the

Father has gifted or called us to do in Him, He has also given us the ability to accomplish it. Another interpretation found in the *Vine's New Testament Dictionary* reads, I have the "freedom of action, or the right to act."[5]

Let us examine several individuals in the Bible who took risks, and a woman who changed the course of history, shifted her position and mind-set, fulfilled God's plan for her, and assisted others in fulfilling their purpose.

1. THE MAN WHO WOULD BE A DELIVERER

Natural talent: Shepherd
Spiritual gift: Pastor of the children of Israel

Tears glistened in the eyes of the mother and daughter as they placed a woven basket in the water in hopes that someone would find the baby boy and protect and care for him. The child was unaware of his surroundings or what his future would hold. He didn't know that one day he would become the powerful deliverer of his people.

Neither did his mother. She only knew that a decree had been issued that all Hebrew male children must be killed! In desperation, she cried out to Jehovah. She had no idea this was all in the plan.

The water dashed against the basket, and the sun illuminated its silhouette as the basket moved slowly downstream. Suddenly, the baby began to cry. The cry was so intense that Pharaoh's daughter heard it as she was preparing to bathe. Cautiously, she walked along the riverside, following the cry. Upon seeing the basket, she quickly beckoned her maid to remove it from the river.

Anxiously she looked inside the delicate, hand-woven basket and saw the beautiful baby. Her heart leaped with joy! She decided to raise the baby as her own son and called him Moses, which means "because I drew him out of the water" (Exod. 2:10).

The child grew and reached manhood. Then one day, God met Moses at a burning bush in Midian to give him his assignment: deliver his people out of slavery in Egypt. He reluctantly accepted the call. "How can I deliver my people out of Egypt and take them to this place called the Promise Land?" he asked.

The risk was great! He felt powerless. Yet God had equipped him for service. He promised to be with him (Heb. 13:5). He went on to address all the excuses Moses gave, all the issues that were preventing him from not accepting his assignment. (See Exodus 2–4.) In the end, Moses led his people, the Israelites, out of slavery in Egypt, and in time they entered the land God promised to give them. He took a risk, trusted God, and as a result, led a nation of people out of bondage and into freedom.

Is the enemy, the evil one, trying to abort the assignment God has given to you? Maybe it is time to reposition. God has need of you to function fully in your gift so that those who are lost and without hope can be found, delivered, and restored.

2. THE YOUNG MAN WHO REFUSED TO LET HIS DESTINY BE THREATENED

Natural Talent: Unknown
Spiritual Gift: Intercession

Note: Though I did not include the gift of intercession with the other gifts of grace in chapter three, it is recognized as a spiritual gift. You can read more about it in Luke 22:41–44; Colossians 1:9–12, and 1 Timothy 2:1–2.

With his hands clenched and his face etched with pain, the young man from the tribe of Judah ran swiftly down the dusty road and suddenly tripped in a patch of tumbleweed. As he untangled himself from the bush, he cried out, "I will never be free. Why did my mother give me such a terrible name, a name that means pain?"

As he buried his face in the weeds, he cried out to Jehovah. Heaven heard his appeal. Jabez's cry was not for riches or vainglory, but for the destiny that lay dormant within him to be revealed. He felt helpless, but he travailed until God granted his request. (See 1 Chronicles 4:9–10.)

Jabez recognized that Jehovah was the only one who could move him from a place of pain to one of power and purpose. So instead of accepting his lot in life, Jabez took the risk to not only desire something different but to ask for it! And God answered. How much have we missed out on simply because we never dared ask the Lord for it? Prayer is powerful. Combined with faith, it will move the heart of the Father.

3. THE WOMAN WHO REFUSED TO BE STATUS QUO

Natural Talent: Secretary
Spiritual Gift: Administration

It was a cold day in December. The sound of the bus door opened and closed as riders boarded and departed the faded yellow city bus. The frost on the windows began to melt as the hum of the heater indicated that waves of heat were being circulated throughout the bus.

A woman sat near the middle of the bus, in the first row of seats designated for black passengers. When white passengers began to crowd the bus, the driver called for her to move to the back of the bus. This woman, whose skin shined like the color of mocha, refused. She was small in stature, but she stood her ground. She had ridden this bus many times before. She knew this driver. He had been rude to her before, and she knew he carried a pistol. Her heart beat rapidly and her palms became sweaty, but she refused to move.[6]

She refused to be status quo but risked being jailed to take a bold stand for what was right. Rosa Parks stood against all odds, and her actions helped launch the civil rights movement of the twentieth century. Today, she is remembered as a woman of courage. She had a clear vision of her purpose and destiny.

OVERCOME THE FEAR OF RISK

The renowned poet Maya Angelou once said, "I believe the most important single thing, beyond discipline and creativity, is daring to dare."[7] All of us, no matter our walk of life, will be called upon to take risks. How will we respond? There are four steps one can take to embrace risk and move toward victory.

1. Be confident in who you are and in Whose you are. Confidence is the opposite of fear. You do not have "a spirit of fear, but of power and of love and of a sound mind" (2 Tim. 1:7). Remember that you have the power to accomplish all things through the Father.

2. Take one step and move with purpose. Movement requires action. Take that first step. If God has given you a specific assignment or plan, He will provide the help or resources you need to be successful. (See 1 Thessalonians 5:24.) Fear is of the enemy, Satan. He desires for you to fail.

3. Pray, as it is the key that unlocks your assignment. Prayer is colorblind, has no boundaries, and sees no status in life. Prayer is for everyone and has many benefits. As you begin to establish a relationship with the Father, you will find that, in His love and generosity, He will unlock the hidden treasures that

belong only to you. Try it. Pray and the fear that has kept you from accomplishing the things God has only for you will begin to diminish until it is gone. Push pass the risks that prevent you from reaching your destiny. When you overcome the risk, you will experience a new level in God, reach new territories that you envision were unconquerable, and experience joy that is unquenchable.

4. Don't try to meet the expectations of others. The expectation of others will often limit our ability to move in our gifts of grace. Worrying about what people will think can be the biggest roadblock when we may already feel insecure or inadequate about moving forward to accomplish that which we are called to do. Putting people's expectation in such a high position in our lives could cause us to abort the plan of God. It shows Him that you trust their words and opinions more than His, that somehow they know your future better than He does.

   Earlier in my ministry, I battled with a spirit of fear because I could not meet man's standard or did not feel free to explore and activate my gifts that the Master has given me because I was concerned about what people would think. This kind of thinking is a trap and leads to wasted years, striving to meet the expectation of others.

   Many people are stuck in jobs that do not bring them fulfillment or joy, while others have never fulfilled their educational desires. All this, because someone told them they are not capable of reaching their goals or they have set their expectations too high.

   However, I challenge you: Step out! Dare to dream again.

If you could, what job would you apply for that you know with assurance you have been called to do? Are you creative? Has anyone said you were analytical? Is further education needed for you to fully function in your skill set? Are you willing to advance? If these and other similar situations fit your story, move forward, contact a career school, ask God for wisdom on how to rethink how you can be more creative or involved in the position you hold. Start with prayer, and start to inquire about what options are available to you. Yes, it may be a risk of courage. Yes, there may be delays. But remember you were created by the biggest risk taker, the Master. Take Him with you. Don't continue to live knowing your assignment is left unfulfilled. You do not want to live with that nagging sense of defeat. Live in a way that will allow you to experience all that God has for you.

THE SUPREME RISK-TAKER

Our Savior made the ultimate sacrifice by giving His life so we could experience abundant living and fulfill our purpose and potential in the earth. Throughout His thirty-three years on earth, Jesus took many risks to do the will of His Father. He was committed to fulfilling His purpose so we could have life and have it more abundantly (John 10:10).

Due to His death, many blessings and unlimited promises are now our inheritance. What do you really have to lose by taking a risk to fulfill your purpose? Don't let fear or doubt keep you from taking that first step toward God's call on your life. Now is a good time for you to revisit the vision God gave you and begin to change your position to fulfill your purpose. It will be worth the risk.

QUESTIONS FOR PERSONAL
AND GROUP REFLECTION

1. Has there ever been a time in your life when you were hesitant to move forward in something that you knew was the right thing for you to do? What held you back? Share the outcome.

2. Is there a fear that is currently keeping you from taking a risk to embrace the call you have been created to fulfill? If so, what is it? Write down the steps you will take to conquer this fear.

3. What are the characteristics of a thief in John 10:10? Share the great promise the Master left us in the latter part of John 10:10. Do you feel excited when you read that we can live abundantly? Why or why not?

MEDITATION FOR TRANSFORMATION

Choose one.

In this chapter, I used Rosa Parks as an example of someone who took a big risk to stand up for what they believe in and to stay committed to their assignment in the face of great opposition. Consider your gift of grace. What risky yet righteous situations can you see your gift calling you to? Would you take the assignment and be willing to take that risk, even if you knew the consequences of that decision would be costly?

Or,

If you are still grappling with opinions of others or any other obstacle mentioned in this chapter, I want to challenge your faith in God ahead of anything else and ask you to write two goals that you wish to accomplish but have not moved to fulfill. Then list two steps needed to meet this goal. As you write, pray. As you pray, allow your spiritual ears to hear God's strategy being revealed to you. He will do it.

YOUR GRACE IN ACTION

Take one step today and begin to fulfill a goal you set at the beginning of the year or even several years ago. Invite someone to walk alongside you to hold you accountable until the goal has been completed. For example, you may desire to return to school, join a Bible study, walk fifteen minutes a day, or develop a resume for a career shift. Remember, this is your life. Take charge of it.

PRAYER OF PARTNERSHIP

Jesus, thank You for Your supreme sacrifice. Help me to realize that in You I have unlimited power and untapped potential. Hebrews 13:5-6 says. "For He Himself has said, 'I will never leave you nor forsake you.' So we may boldly say: 'The Lord is my helper; I will not fear. What can man do to me?'" I am not alone. You are always with me. Amen.

Chapter Five

HIDDEN IN THE HOUSE

IN EACH CONGREGATION there are members who are hidden. Some members hide by choice because they carry the scars from a previous hurt from another church. A few members do not wish to be held accountable or disagree with the leader's vision. Others hide because they have a fear of being called upon to participate. The ones that remain are hidden in the house by God as they wait for the right time to be revealed. The word *hidden* means "concealed, obscure, or covert."[1]

Churches today are oftentimes challenged and struggle to keep members active and involved regardless of the programs offered. Every member is part of the body and is vital to the growth. When we all work together, we will function as one and have a healthy and vibrant church.

CHURCH AS HOME AND FAMILY

Think about your childhood home. Regardless of the number of people who lived in the home—one or ten, Uncle V, Aunt See, or Cousin May—you were family. It may have been an apartment, boarding house, or temporary shelter, but it was home. There may have been one member who you have not seen for years, hidden from the family, or the "odd one" who always had their own way of doing things, but you are all still family!

The church is also a family that consists of members with various needs and who come from diverse cultures, socioeconomic backgrounds, and have various learning abilities and styles. With all these differences, the goal I believe God has for us is that we learn to be accepting and embrace each other because we are of one body. God has gifted each believer with a talent or gift. To fulfill God's plan in the earth and to reach the lost and dying, each member's gift must be discovered, developed, and released so that they can go into their communities and spheres of influence to manifest the power and glory of God.

THE PASTOR SETS THE ATMOSPHERE

As the visionary, the shepherd or pastor has the unique responsibility to give spiritual nourishment, protection, and unconditional love to the members who sit under their leadership. It is crucial that the pastor fulfills this mission because the spiritual growth and development of each member is vital for the church's success. Since the church has a diverse membership, the pastor must prayerfully seek how to cultivate the members who are hidden, within his or her congregation, so their purpose will be fulfilled as well as being a healthy contributor to the body of Christ.

Some members are hidden for various reasons as was shared earlier in this chapter, yet others are hidden to be revealed at the appointed time to save many people in the Kingdom of God.

A pastor should help members identify and nurture the gifts God has given them, and help them find ways to use it to minister to the body. Jesus set forth the gifts of grace in the body of Christ that have been distributed to each member (Rom. 12:6), and every believer is commanded to use their gifts within the body of Christ.

It is such a great privilege for the shepherd or the designated leadership to understand the call and gifts bestowed upon their membership and assist them in their spiritual growth, for the equipping of the saints for the work of ministry and the edifying of the body of Christ (Eph. 4:12). When we negate or disallow the gifts or allow only a few to operate and say, "We do not see a need for the gifts in our church," we have said, we do not need to equip the saints or members within our body for the work of the ministry. We do not follow God's plan to save the lost for the kingdom of God. The members are at risk of being underdeveloped and not being active as God purposed us.

When the gifts are fully activated, the leader will sense a shift of excitement in the body of believers, and the church will begin to move into a higher kingdom dimension where the members will earnestly seek God and His way of doing things. As a result, they will become committed to sharing the good news of the gospel to their community, providing food to the hungry, extending hope to those who are without hope, bringing deliverance to those who are bound, laying hands on the sick and seeing them recover, and more.

BECOMING AN EFFECTIVE TEAM MEMBER

In his book *Ministering Spiritual Gifts*, Dr. Bill Hamon, says, "Every saint has a membership ministry."[2]

Membership ministry defines a church or body of believers. It is when each member is actively working in their designated gift of grace but still working and moving as one unit. Peter pens in his first epistle, "As each one has a gift, minister it to one another, as good stewards of the manifold of grace" (1 Pet. 4:10).

To maintain good spiritual health and fulfill our purpose, we must recognize and accept responsibility and accountability within the body to function as one. Here are four ways we can be healthy and effective members in the body of Christ:

1. We must honor God. To honor God is to be obedient to His voice, His Word, and our leader, who follows Him.

2. We must have a servant's heart. Mark 10:43–44 says, "Whosoever will be great among you, shall be your minister: and whosoever of you will be the chiefest, shall be servant of all" (KJV).

3. We must commit to be faithful and protect the spiritual gift(s) we have been given.

4. We must prepare to be equipped, to exercise our gifts, and be ready to activate or mobilize our spiritual gifts under our leaders, as God has mandated us to do.

PLANTED FOR A SEASON

Perennials are my favorite plants. They grow each year without needing to be replanted. Other plants are called annuals and need to be replanted each year. Each group has distinct characteristics and qualities, just like the members who are planted in a church body. It is interesting to note that some perennials have to be slightly hidden or placed in a shady area where the sun is very low to produce a healthy plant.

All members are planted within their church to mature in their Christian walk and to receive knowledge through the Word of God. As you mature through the Word, you will discover your gifts and be trained and equipped on how to use them.

Some members are planted within their church for a specific season to fulfill a certain assignment they have been called to do by God through their leader. For example, you have discovered that your gift of grace is helps. The pastor has also recognized and identified your passion and love for those who are in need and desire to see their lives enriched. He has given you a special ministry assignment to coordinate a community outreach for the church. You have been activated or released to go forth in your specific call.

Activation means more than just to be mobilized. The preparation you have received through leadership who have trained and equipped you is one of trust and one that helps you to carry out your assignment effectively. This special assignment is for a designated time until other members are trained and equipped to carry on when the time comes for your release.

Unfortunately, when members leave their assignment before God releases them, it affects their growth as well as the growth and flourishing of the body of Christ because we are one. Some members become discontent and disappointed because the assignment is not glamorous. Others may become discouraged because the assignment is not flourishing as they anticipated.

If God has directed you to accept a spiritual call or assignment, He will always equip, train, provide for, sustain, and guide you until the assignment is completed. I would encourage you to never leave an assignment until you have been released by God. However, there are some emergency instances—spiritual, physical, financial, interpersonal, or otherwise—that occur where we must pray about whether to stay or leave.

If you have been called to work as a missionary minister in a Third-World country, you have to be aware of the culture of that country. If you sense danger and it is not safe for you and your family to remain, consult God, along with your leader who can assist you with the proper protocol for departure. Another example may be if, during your assignment, conflict arises between you and your spiritual leader. Do not immediately abandon what God has called you to do.

Pause and pray. Demonstrate a spirit of love and humility and ask God's assistance to resolve the conflict. God knows our hearts and intensions for the purpose He has called us to accomplish.

No matter where you are planted as a member, challenges may come.

HOW DID I GET HERE?

Generally the first question a believer might ask when they face roadblocks or hindrances as they earnestly wait to be released to go forth with the call God has on their life is, "How did I get here?" They may feel certain limitations have been set by their leader as they sat waiting hidden in the house to prevent them from being unveiled. The word *unveiled* means to "to reveal or disclose by or as if by removing a veil or covering; to unveil a secret; to unveil a truth."[3] Therefore, as you wait to be released into your call or gifting, there are things you can do to prepare for the unveiling.

1. Spend time in the Word of God and meditate on His promises. God's Word reveals His will for our lives. As we read and meditate daily, we will gain confidence that when the time of unveiling occurs, we will walk out in boldness.

2. Stay in prayer. This will keep you grounded and not allow the enemy and his imps to bring distractions that cause you to release yourself or step ahead of God before the appointed time.

3. Continue to mature and strengthen your character. One of the fruit of the Spirit is temperance. This is a form of self-control with which many individuals struggle in their Christian walk. If this fruit is

not controlled, it can prevent one from completing their assignment and fulfilling their destiny. Apply the same principles above to defeat this by spending time in the Word of God and praying to conquer this stronghold.

4. Continue to be faithful where you are planted. At times, you may experience frustration, but if God has placed you where you are, remain faithful in your assignment there and your time to be unveiled (elevated or promoted) will come.

THE WOUNDED MEMBER

At the beginning of this chapter, we gave several reasons why members are hidden in the church. One of the reasons is that they may have experienced hurt from another member or a leader. No church member is exempt from being wounded or offended. Dale A. Robbins writes in his book *How to Keep from Getting Hurt in Church*:

Unfortunately, the church has sometimes been a place where many have experienced wounds instead of healing. In fact, statistics show that a great percentage of persons who cease attending church, do so because of some type of offense or injury to their feelings that happened there. Sometimes these occur because of the insensitivity of the church; other times, people are themselves at fault for being too touchy or sensitive to misunderstandings.[4]

Jesus told the disciples (apostles) that they would be offended: "Woe to the world because of offenses! For offenses must come, but woe to that man by whom the offense comes!" (Matt. 18:7). Jesus took the worst offense! Nevertheless, He didn't let it stop Him. As the Savior, He understood His mission and the need to fulfill His destiny.

Praise God! We too can fulfill our purpose. It does not matter how the enemy, Satan, attempts to put us at risk. We will complete that which God has called us forth to do. When we battle with affliction, doubt, or defeat, we have to know who we are and whose we are in Christ so we can keep moving forward.

In his book *The Bait of Satan,* John Bevere writes that "offense is a potential trap" that every believer will encounter as they endeavor to fulfill their purpose or walk in their ministry or call.[5] This is what happened when Jesus visited His hometown of Nazareth. He was rejected when He tried to minister there. As He taught in the temple, many were amazed and said, "'Where did this Man get this wisdom and these mighty works? Is this not the carpenter's son? Is not His mother called Mary?...Where then did this Man get all these things?'" (Matt. 13:54–56). They were offended by Him (Matt. 13:57), and He wasn't able to perform any miracles there.

Once offense takes root, it can seem almost impossible to eradicate. Reading and confessing the Word of God daily is the one sure way to destroy the stronghold of offense. I invite you to read the story about Cheri and how the spirit of rejection, a type of offense, almost prevented her from fulfilling her purpose. Her pastor showed unconditional love and sensitivity toward her plight and redirected her to think of another way to bless others with her gift of worship.

WHERE DO I FIT?

Cheri had been a believer for one year and attended a church where the gifts of grace were welcomed and exercised. As a new believer, she had discovered that one of her gifts was worship.[6] She was extremely excited to use her gift to bless others because she felt so much joy when she sang.

One Sunday, during the morning service, an announcement

was read that several new members were needed for the worship team. The description and expectations were given, and Cheri knew immediately that she would fit this role. Eagerly, she signed up with the anticipation of being chosen. She prepared diligently for the audition, confident that she would be selected.

On the day of the tryouts, her name was called. She stepped forward, whispered a silent prayer, and began to sing. A spirit of praise began to well up in her belly as she sensed the anointing flow from her head to her feet. She knew God was with her.

Several days later, the results were posted. Her name was not listed as one of the new worship team members. Cheri was devastated! She met all the qualifications and her performance was anointed. She contacted the leader immediately to find out why she was not chosen. He shared with her that there were many participants who applied and only two positions were filled. He encouraged her to continue to try and at the right timing, it would happen for her. In her heart, she knew she would not try again. It was not meant for her to use her gift of grace to be part of the worship team at her church.

For several weeks, Cheri was unable to attend church due to a feeling of hurt and a spirit of rejection. As a young believer, she was unaware of the enemy and his deceptive strategies to prevent her from going to church. She cried out to God and asked Him to take the pain away.

The next day she received a call from her pastor who expressed his concern about how she was missed at church and offered his assistance. Cheri shared with him how she had tried out for a worship team position and was not selected. The pastor asked if he could pray with her. She wept as he prayed. She thanked him for the prayer and his call. He encouraged her to hold on and be faithful in the spiritual things of God, and in time she would be promoted.

He suggested that she attend the children's church and help them with their worship service, teaching the children how important worship is to God.

In closing, he asked if she would consider going with the ministry team to assist with worship at the local nursing home. He further encouraged her by saying, "The ministry leader has not been successful in finding anyone to assist in this needed area and your help will be greatly appreciated."

Cheri repented and asked God to forgive her for feeling rejected. Suddenly, she experienced peace as never before and knew that God's desire for her was to use her gift to bless others. She knew now that the Lord had another open door for her to be used in worship. She was excited to learn about the two positions that the pastor shared with her and moved forward to seek more information.

Have you ever felt like Cheri? Have you ever been waiting to be unveiled, expecting your gift to be discovered, recognized, and to be released? There is a *kairos* time and opportunity to move your seat. Your seat is your unique place of ministry where God will position you to bless others. God may have you hidden for such a time as this. What time is it? It is a time where revival is breaking out throughout the land, a harvest of souls is seeking to find hope in their time of despair. Did you know the Master is equipping you within the body of Christ to be prepared to save and deliver many people through the call He has placed on your life?

TIMING IS EVERYTHING

Wait on your timing. Genesis 16:3-4 illustrates how man's plan attempts to usurp God's prophetic assignment on an individual's life. God had promised to give Abraham and his wife, Sarah, a child even though Sarah was well beyond child-bearing age. After waiting for years for God to send their promised child, Sarah told Abraham to take her handmaid,

Hagar, as his wife and have a child with her. God had not forgotten Sarah and His promise to give her a child, but she and Abraham chose to move out of His timing.

God keeps His promises. He does not lie or change His mind. If He said it, it will come to pass. If there is something God has promised you that has not come to fruition, do not give up. Expect it any day. It will come.

In the right season, God's promise to Abraham and Sarah came to pass. Sarah birthed the promised child, Isaac. Her dream to have a child was fulfilled. Unfortunately, Hagar was the victim in this situation. Her son, Ishmael, was not the child God promised to Abraham. To this day Ishmael's descendants, the Arab people, are at odds with the Jewish people, who are the descendants of Abraham's promised son, Isaac. Moving out of God's timing never ends well.

Only God can take you to places in Him that you have never been but have always wanted to go. As always, you want to be under the authority of a leader designated to cover and protect you as you gather momentum to do *great exploits* in the kingdom of God. (See Daniel 11:32.)

If you are a member in a church where the spiritual gifts are not fully received or exercised, pray about how God wants to use you to bless the body. Again, I say, be prayerful! Share with your spiritual leader your gift and seek spiritual insight to be properly released in your gift or call. If God has placed you there, be faithful until you get a clear signal from God to be released to move on. The Scripture says, "Let us not be weary in well doing: for in due season we shall reap, if we faint not" (Gal. 6:9, KJV).

In his book *The Bait of Satan*, John Bevere admonishes his readers:

When God sends you to a place or ministry do not leave until God releases you. If the Lord is silent, He is often saying, "Don't change a thing. Do not leave. Stay where

I have placed you. When God does instruct you to leave, you will go out with peace, no matter what the condition of the ministry."[7]

QUESTIONS FOR PERSONAL AND GROUP REFLECTION

1. Have you ever felt hidden in a congregation? Are you free to share what led to you being hidden? Were you unveiled by choice? At what time were you unveiled or your gift discovered?

2. Is there a time where you went ahead of God, took things in your own hands and should have waited? Was that experience painful?

3. We all have been offended at one time or another. Yet offense will prevent you from moving forward to fulfill your kingdom assignment. Will you begin to release whoever has offended you or address the reason the offense has come? Pray and bless the offender or those who have offended you. Now begin your new journey.

MEDITATION FOR TRANSFORMATION

What would you do if you had a spiritual gift and were unable to exercise it or it was not recognized? Write your comments or thoughts in a journal or a notepad.

YOUR GRACE IN ACTION

List the kinds of offenses you have faced in your life (lies, ill-treatment, and the like). Spend some time in prayer, forgive, and release all the individuals who have offended you. Next, begin to bless those individuals until you sense a release in your spirit. Be honest. Some offenses may have occurred in your childhood, others in your high school years, and some in your church after you became an adult. Press in until you actually get a breakthrough. Last, begin to praise God for the release. Do not stop until you have victory. Receive God's healing grace over you right now, in Jesus's name.

PRAYER OF PARTNERSHIP

Thank You, Jesus, for reaching down and pulling me out of the obscure places where I have been hiding. I am now free to exercise my gifts of grace. My leader or pastor has released me to walk in covenant victory to accomplish all that the Master has for me. I will no longer feel ashamed, carry condemnation, have low self-esteem, or carry any inferiority trait that prevents me from fulfilling all that You have for me. I am free! Amen.

Chapter Six

YOUR ANOINTING IS TOO COSTLY FOR YOU TO REMAIN QUIET

SHE HEARD THE rustling of the trees as she walked swiftly across the cobblestones, leaves crushing underfoot, to reach the house of Simon the Pharisee. Under her garment, she clutched an alabaster box of costly oil to anoint this man they called the Teacher. It didn't matter that she hadn't been invited to dinner. "They must let me in," she thought.

She knocked on the door. A small man with piercing eyes cracked it open and glared at her. "You're not on the guest list," he replied with a look of contempt.

"I came to see the Teacher," she said, determination etched on her face.

As He reclined at the table, the Teacher saw her silhouette at the door and said to Simon, "Let her in!"

Still not too happy to have this unexpected guest, Simon beckoned her to come in. She walked slowly over to the Teacher, stood behind Him, and began to weep. As her tears wet His feet, she stooped down, dried the tears with her hair, kissed His feet, and poured fragrant oil on them.

As Simon witnessed this, he thought, *"If this man really was a prophet, He would know what kind of woman has touched Him. She is a sinner!"*

The Teacher knew this woman's heart, and He began to share a spiritual truth with Simon and his guests through a parable about unforgiveness. He concluded His story by telling Simon, "You invited me to dinner, yet you offered me no water to wash my feet. Nor did you kiss Me or anoint My head." (See Luke 7:36–47.) He then turned to the woman and said, "Your sins are forgiven.... Your faith has saved you. Go in peace" (Luke 7:48, 50).

THE ESSENCE OF HIS
FRAGRANCE—THE ANOINTING

This woman had risked all to see the man called Teacher. Nothing—not the whispers, scoffers, finger-pointers, sooth-sayers, or even previous relationships—could keep her from her mission. The alabaster box of oil the woman clutched tightly was her most costly possession, yet she was unaware that it represented the essence of the Teacher's fragrance, the anointing, and the key to gain access to her destiny. She was desperate to see and touch this Man who had the power to set her free and change her position from a place of pain to one of purpose.

Are you desperate to get close to Jesus, the Teacher? Do you want to know Him better? If so, pursue Him until you discover who He is and all that God has for you. It will be worth the effort. When you encounter Him and embrace His essence, the anointing, you will begin to witness and demonstrate signs, wonders, and miracles.

WHAT IS THE ANOINTING?

Chriō, the Greek word translated *anointing*, means "to smear or rub with oil...anoint."[1] Timothy Stokes, pastor of Family Worship Center Church in Flint, Michigan, defines the anointing as "the ability of God working in and through humans to perform His Word."[2] The anointed oil is also used as a symbol of the anointing, and there are several uses for it. One way the anointing oil is used is at a holy conse-cration or ordination service where the spiritual leaders or presbytery will pour the anointed oil over the individuals heads who desire to dedicate and consecrate their lives to ministry. This will be followed by the laying on of hands with prayer. Pastor Stokes goes on to say, "The anointing that comes upon a person, enabling them to minister to others in need, is supposed to be administered in a spirit of selflessness and love."[3]

As a result, the purpose for the anointing is to minister and serve. Luke, the physician, clearly defines the purpose of what the anointing does: "The Spirit of the Lord is upon me, Because He has anointed Me to preach the gospel to the poor; He has sent Me to heal the brokenhearted, to proclaim liberty to the captives, and recovery of sight to the blind, to set at liberty those who are oppressed" (Luke 4:18).

When it rests upon you, it will bring the unction (or the anointing) to encourage, empower, and help others. It is not to be used to impress others or for vainglory. The anointing is given to glorify God. As you walk in the anointing, it will move you out of the ordinary way of doing things to walk in the supernatural.

Faith is a key ingredient that works (energizes or stimulates) the anointing. When an individual sits in a service where the anointing is present and the minister speaks forth a word of healing, the person will reach out through faith, unwavering, and receive their immediate healing they had been seeking for years. You may ask, "How did this happen?" I believe the individual who received the healing had been praying, believing, expecting, and confessing God's promises when the Master met them at their moment of need.

Every believer can carry the anointing; however, your relationship with Him will affect how the anointing will flow through you to others. God desires His children to have pure hearts and committed lives where He can use you to change the lives of men, women, and children who see no hope.

THE ANOINTING CREATES CHANGE

In June 2012, I attended the IMPACT Network Global Conference held in Merrillville, Indiana, hosted by John Eckhardt, apostle/pastor of Crusaders Ministries, Chicago, Illinois. From that time until now, my worship experience has never been the same. Approximately one-thousand or more workshop participants filled the auditorium with their hands lifted and voices blended in worship. It was as if an invitation was sent to heaven inviting the King into their midst.

Suddenly, the atmosphere changed, and I knew Jesus had walked into the room. His presence released the anointing. It was indescribable! People began to weep, some rocked and moaned, and others lay prostrate at the altar and throughout the room. Some were healed, and others delivered.

Everything stopped when the King walked in. Flesh became silent, and an open portal from heaven released answers to the prayer petitions that we had been bringing before God. Many lives were transformed that day because the leader was sensitive to the anointing that creates change. It was later discovered that the gifts of grace began to flow within the service, and ministries were birthed.

Do you remember a time when the Master walked into a situation that had been challenging or burdening you and suddenly everything changed? When we allow the Master to govern our daily lives and places of worship, we will experience that kingdom dimension that will allow prophetic revelation to flow. Expect Him to show up anytime and anywhere when the anointing is present.

THE ANOINTING IS COSTLY

The anointing is priceless. A monetary value cannot be placed upon it. It is for a divine purpose. When one has the mantle of anointing, it is like the precious ointment that the woman carried in the alabaster box that was worth one year's wages. She embraced it as if one precious drop would spill to the ground, her chance to be free from the past and walk in victory would be at risk. Ultimately, she would be left unprotected and exposed again to walk in a life filled with despair.

In his book *How to Walk in the Supernatural Power of God*, Guillermo Maldonado, apostle/pastor defines a mantle as "a loose sleeveless garment worn over other clothes. A figurative cloak symbolizing preeminence or authority in the spiritual realm, as the glory, kindness, lordship, excellence, nobility, authority, strength, essence, and great courage."[4]

When one walks with the anointing, it will cost you something. It may cost you friends who don't understand the passion and joy you receive through the anointing as you see others who are bound, set free. It may cost you to step out of your comfort zone and begin a prayer walk through your neighborhood with another believer to extend hope to those who see no way out. It may lead you to speak to the gang leader about another way of living.

Whatever the cost, with the anointing, we will gain more than we will lose. We will experience the peace of God, boldness in our faith, courage, power, and much more. When we yield to God's plan to serve others, release them from the things that have held them captive, and give them the opportunity to fulfill God's plan for their lives, it will be life-changing.

THE ANOINTING IS NOT QUIET

The anointing cannot be restricted when it is released. As you faithfully commit to God and remain open to what His desire is for you, He will send you to places you never thought you would go. Ask God to use you for His glory. When He does, those you touch who were blind will say, "I was once blind, but now I can see." Others may say, "Thank you! I once was sick, but now I am healed!"

The End-Time revival is spreading like spiritual fire through our cities, nation, and world. The Master desires to use you to release your loved ones from the grip of Satan. Furthermore, you are needed to gather the harvest for the kingdom of God. We can no longer be in our own world with the windows closed and shades drawn. You can no longer be quiet. Walk in your anointing and help others fulfill God's best for their lives.

THE ANOINTING CHANGED MY LIFE

In 2011, I had a strong desire to learn more about the gift of grace called prophecy. Apostle Paul encouraged the believer who desires this gift by saying, "Having then gifts differing according to the grace that is given to us, let us use them; if prophecy, let us prophesy in proportion to our faith..." (Rom. 12:6). I began to pray and ask God how to receive this gift because it wasn't something I could teach myself; it is a gift that comes from Him to be "distributed individually as He wills" (1 Cor. 12:11).

I received an invitation in June of that year to attend a ministry graduation ceremony. When I arrived and was seated, my eyes were drawn to a woman seated on the pulpit that I had not seen since high school. As the ceremony progressed, I realized that she was the graduation speaker.

When it was time for her to speak, the woman went to the microphone and gave the proper acknowledgments. As she looked out over the audience, her eyes lit on me. She asked me to come to the front. At first, I was hesitant and sat there for a minute. She called for me again. This time, I walked up the aisle, and stood at the pulpit.

The woman asked my name. Then she began to share with the congregation that she had not seen me since childhood.

She asked me if she could minister to me. I consented. The words she spoke were unfamiliar to me, but God spoke to me through her. It was as if she had lived with me since my youth.

She spoke to my spirit. I felt the tears well up and begin to fall. I did not want to weep openly, but she spoke to my hurt, the disappointments, the promises yet to be fulfilled, and my future. She prophetically spoke about my past and gave a prophetic word about my present and future. After this, she paused for a moment and began to sing a melody to me. As she concluded, she told me of the things God had for me that were still left to be accomplished. The publishing of this book with my name as the author is one of the words of prophecy spoken that was to be fulfilled.

She asked if she could place her hand on my shoulder and pray.

I nodded my head, "Yes."

Immediately, I felt the anointing of God being imparted from her to me. Suddenly, the brokenness that had been residing in my heart for such a long time began to mend and a spirit of freedom and courage began to arise. At that moment, I knew God had more for me and understood why I sensed the urgency to attend the ministry graduation ceremony.

Did you know that God will use circumstances, people, and places to orchestrate and fulfill His plan for you? As a result of the anointing that rested on me that evening, the Master encouraged me to go forth with boldness and find a safe place where I would be accepted and supported to become equipped, trained, and released by leadership to go forth and walk in my destiny to help others discover and fulfill their purpose in the kingdom of God.

The words the woman ministered to me were truly from God. Since then, the purpose of her prophetic words are being fulfilled in my life, in part, and the second part of what she said will be revealed in time. Praise God for His faithfulness.

FOR SUCH A TIME AS THIS

Esther opened the curtains to look onto the outer court. Birds were chirping, and the sun was hidden behind the clouds. It would have been a lovely day for a stroll, if only she didn't have so much weighing on her heart.

Her birth name was Hadassah, but everyone called her Esther because no one knew she was Jewish. This was her uncle Mordecai's idea. When she became part of the king's harem, he had instructed her to not tell anyone of her heritage. Mordecai had been like a father to her after her parents died, so she obeyed his request.

Esther had distinguished herself above all the other women seeking to catch the king's attention, and now she was queen. However, that didn't mean her life was a fairy tale. Esther had been distressed ever since her uncle told her about the decree. Haman intended to annihilate her people. He hated the Jews, and he hated her uncle even more, because he would bow only to Jehovah and not to him, a mere man.

Mordecai insisted that Esther talk to her husband, King Ahasuerus, and plead for the lives of their people. He told her, "If you keep quiet at a time like this, God will deliver the Jews from some other source, but you and your relatives will die; what's more, who can say but that God has brought you into the palace for just such a time as this?" (Esther 4:14, TLB).

It was forbidden for anyone, including Queen Esther, to go in to see the king unless invited. Nevertheless, Esther told her uncle: "Go, gather all the Jews that are present in Susa, and observe a fast for me; do not eat or drink for three days, night or day. I and my maids also will fast in the same way. Then I will go in to [see] the king [without being summoned], which is against the law; and if I perish, I perish" (Esther 4:16, AMP).

After three days had passed, Esther put on her royal robes and took slow steps to the king's palace. She held her breath as she walked inside. Upon seeing her, the king extended his scepter. Finally able to exhale, Esther approached him and made her request.

In the end, the king spared the lives of her people, and Haman was killed instead. Deliverance did come to the Jews, and Esther was the individual God chose to bring that victory. A young girl who had been hidden was used of God to save a nation of people.

Esther had to be bold and risk death to go before the king. But she was willing to do so. She surrounded herself with people who would support her and fast with her for God's favor to accomplish the task.

The anointing Esther carried as a deliverer for her people changed their future and reversed the order that had been decreed against them. She chose to walk in this anointing, and her people were not destroyed. Her anointing empowered her to do miracles from her God, Jehovah. He gave her the boldness, strength, and insight to accomplish her mission and save her people. The Lord chose Esther for this special assignment and anointed her for this work because she stepped forward at a time when she saw the need was great. The personal relationship she had with Jehovah and her desire to consecrate herself through fasting and prayer gave her the spiritual power she needed as she went in and stood before the king. By her faith and action, the Lord gave her favor with the king and her petition was granted. Esther knew where to go in that moment when the lives of her people were on the line. She knew her God would not fail her.

Perhaps God is raising you up for such a time as this and, like Esther, He is calling you to be a deliverer in this

End-Time season. Just as it was in Esther's day, lives hang in the balance of your obedience. How will you respond?

YOUR ASSIGNMENT WILL REQUIRE THE ANOINTING

As a member within the body of Christ, you will need to carry the anointing of God in your everyday life. Without the anointing, you cannot successfully fulfill the plan God has called you to. If your desire is to return to school and finish your education, you can carry the anointing to release a timely word to your classmate who is at the point of giving up and walking away from the purpose she or he has been called forth to do.

As Esther was called to carry out her mission to save her people, what will the anointing empower you to do in your sphere of influence? Be ready and available to move in the anointing at a moment's notice! God has called you for such a time as this.

QUESTIONS FOR PERSONAL AND GROUP REFLECTION

1. Describe a time when God used your gift to bless someone through the anointing you carry?

2. How did your actions affect the person you ministered to?

3. Has there ever been a quiet time where you felt the anointing to get up or go to an individual and pray with them or leave an encouraging word with them? What experience did the individual receive from your obedience to move at the anointing?

MEDITATION FOR TRANSFORMATION

As I shared in this chapter, the anointing will cost you something. Will you list one thing in your journal or notepad that you have lost by carrying the anointing?

YOUR GRACE IN ACTION

This week, find a believer to share thoughts about the anointing and how it has changed their life. For example, ask what is their definition of the anointing? Then study and cross-reference the word *anointing* in another Bible translation. Allow a new meaning to open up to you. Consider using this study to initiate a Bible study group with friends.

PRAYER OF PARTNERSHIP

Thank You, Jesus, for resting Your anointing upon me so that I may bless others. I never want to lose the anointing that will set others free. Amen.

Chapter Seven

YOUR SEAT OF DESTINY

God has uniquely gifted you to accomplish a specific task. You may be God's best-kept secret, but He doesn't want you to remain hidden forever. He wants you to discover and move into all He has for you as His child. God wants you to learn about the gifts of grace He has given you, so He can activate and release you to walk in them. You have unlimited potential in God, and you walk with an anointing that is too costly for you to remain quiet. When those truths become a reality in your life, you will find yourself at your seat of destiny.

It is not usual for the special or unique place of ministry to which you've been called to be referred to as a seat of destiny. That is how the Lord revealed it to me. I see that as the people of God are seated in heavenly places, we rule and reign from this seat in the Spirit according to the call within which we minister and serve through our gifts of grace. Let's take a closer look.

The root word of destiny is *destine*. The word *destine* is defined as "to be set-apart by design for a future use or purpose."[1] Your seat is not for everyone but designed with you in mind. Each individual has to walk out their purpose and fulfill the call God has created them to do. Your seat of destiny may be directed in many ways to be used in the kingdom of God. The following are just a few assignments you may be called to perform within your gift of grace.

- You may be called or sent out to serve others as they move forward to fulfill their ministry call. (Example: missions ministry, assist with a new church planted in another region, or provide guidance for a group of ministries within a territory)

- You may be called to fulfill a leadership role within your church or community. (Example: as an outreach ministry coordinator who will instruct and guide new members on how to care and support those in need, as a transportation assistant director, who will prepare new volunteers to safeguard children and youth for field trips and school events; or as workshop facilitator, who provides training to a group of single mothers and fathers on budgeting)

- You may be called to the marketplace, your sphere of influence where a word of faith and hope can be sown into others with the spoken word. (Example: college chaplain, ambassador, or political leadership role)

THE PURPOSE OF YOUR SEAT OF DESTINY

For we are God's workmanship, created in Christ Jesus to do good works, which God prepared in advance for us to do.

—EPHESIANS 2:10

The writer of the book of Ephesians, Apostle Paul, has distinguished us as works of art. Isn't it amazing that we are God's masterpieces? He created us in His own image (Gen. 1:27). Before the world was formed, God had us on His mind. Therefore, if we are God's works of art, He knew the talents and gifts we were created with and the exact ones for which we are best suited. Our steps have been ordered by Him. It is our time to move forward and occupy our seats of destiny.

The renowned and gifted Italian artist Leonardo da Vinci created the oil painting masterpiece *Mona Lisa*. Although many have never seen the original piece, located in the Louvre in Paris, it is known for its beauty worldwide. It was also noted that da Vinci was not only an artist, but also he was a scientist, inventor and doctor."[2]

Your seat of destiny or ministry position is not only for you but for the kingdom of God. The kingdom is where the Master rules and has dominion. It is where His way of doing things is superior.

Did you know that because of your seat of destiny, God gave you the power and authority to set things in order? (See Luke 9:1–2.) You have also been given the power as His disciple (or student) to fulfill the Great Commission (Mark 16:15–17) and to resist your enemy, Satan, when he tries to detour you from reaching your unique place of ministry. Use your spiritual authority at the gate of access to resist him.

THE GATE OF ACCESS

Throughout the Old and New Testament, gates are frequently mentioned. They are symbolic of spiritual authority. They also represent a place where leaders met and gave counsel. Gates also symbolize protection. In the Torah (the first five books of the Old Testament), the gate was where community action took place, similar to our marketplace. In the gates of a city, laws were decreed and judgment was passed.[3]

In the spirit realm, there are gates where we sit as leaders in the kingdom of God, and, through our prayers and gifts of grace, we administrate the laws and culture of God's kingdom. It is from our seats of destiny that we bind on earth what is bound in heaven and we loose on earth what is loosed in heaven and use the keys of the kingdom to exercise our authority given by Jesus Christ himself. (See Matthew 16:19; 28:18.)

Your seat of destiny is situated at the gate that gives you access to the power you need to influence, motivate, and encourage others. Accept the authority and power you have been given by the Master. They are available to you on earth anytime and anywhere. Begin to mobilize. You must have the confidence to walk boldly and begin to walk in your authority.

By activating your position at the gate, you declare to the Lord your confidence in how He has equipped and anointed you. You have the power and authority to take hold of any hindrance or defeatism that would prevent you or the ones you serve to move forward and fulfill the plans the Master has for you and them. The enemy will endeavor to prevent us from taking territories for the kingdom and from gathering the harvest of souls. However, as you take your seat of destiny at the gate of access, you will learn to use your authority in the body, the marketplace, and beyond.

MARKETPLACE EXPERIENCE

The marketplace is one of your spheres of influence. It is a place where daily connections, networking, conversations, and interactions take place. It is our neighborhoods, shopping and business centers, public libraries, grocery stores, workplaces, and more.

The word marketplace has been used interchangeably with gate. In biblical times, it represented a place where the individual would buy, sell, and barter goods, just as manufacturers and some consumers do in the marketplace today. This is especially seen during the harvest time of fruits and vegetables sold at state fairs. The farmer's markets in our communities where the "market stalls" were also placed out-side the gate for vendors to sell their goods.[4]

Each day we have marketplace opportunities to share our gifts and call. Did you know that your gifts are needed even more to fulfill the Great Commission during this End-Time season and to serve the kingdom (Mark 16:14)? God is a spirit. He needs your voice to share His love and promises to indi-viduals who are in bondage with addictions. He needs your feet to walk into houses of ill repute and extend a hand of compassion to those who feel there is no way out. Ultimately, we are commissioned to share the good news that His saving grace will empower and transform them.

May I challenge you to listen intently to hear the Master's voice when He calls you to shift from a place of complacency to a position of urgency so that you may more effectively apply your gifts of grace to serve others with confidence and humility? Will you step out with me to make a difference in the marketplace and to bless others and create change? You can encourage a neighbor who has lost a loved one, speak faith to someone who feels rejected, and provide resources to a single mom or a widow who lives on a limited income. These, and others within our sphere of influence, can be blessed with our gift.

Much has been written in the Bible about the three-and-a-half years Jesus spent in ministry. During that time, He knew no stranger. His gifts preceded Him as He walked throughout the cities and countryside. Not only did He teach the Beatitudes, heal the sick, and feed the multitudes, but also He sat, ate, and talked with those in His market-place, such as the tax collector, Zacchaeus, whose life was transformed in His presence. (See Luke 19:5–10.)

God has called us to the marketplace. He wants us to "go out into the highways and hedges, and compel them to come in, that [His] house may be filled" (Luke 14:23). He distributed the gifts of grace to believers so we can serve and extend faith so lives will be changed and hope restored to a lost and dying world.

THE MASTER'S SIGNATURE IS ON YOUR PAPERWORK

This is a powerful story of a man named Nehemiah who was confident in his God. He sought Jehovah through prayer that his employer's, King Artaxerxes, heart would be receptive of his request to take a leave of absence to go and rebuild the walls and gates of Jerusalem that were in ruins. As a cup-bearer to the king, he held a vital role to taste the king's wine before he drank it, to prevent anyone from poisoning him. Ultimately, he risked his life for his employer. So, really, his leaving his position even for a short time could put the king's life in danger, if there were not trustworthy backup. I imagine that the king and his advisors were hesitant to grant Nehemiah's request.

In addition to requesting a leave of absence, Nehemiah asked the king if he would give him letters with his signature for the governors of the region beyond the river, which would permit him to pass through till he reached Judah. An additional letter was needed for Asaph, keeper of the king's forest, to request that timber be provided for his house and the "beams for the gates of the citadel which pertains to the temple, for the city wall." King Artaxerxes consented. (See Nehemiah 2:3–9.)

Do you know that you have God's signature on your paperwork to move forward with your gift of grace? The paperwork is not a literal piece of paper with His written signature, but His Spirit within you and His blood that was shed on the Cross approves you and commissions you to go forth! They are your signatures of approval.

If you have been trained, equipped, activated, and released to move forward in your gift of grace, what's stopping you?

Whether you use your gifting and calling within your faith community or outside the walls to travel into unknown cities, states, or even as you cross the ocean to nations, the urgency builds that the Master has need of you.

Is the spirit of fear still hovering over you? Resist it, and it shall go. (See James 4:7.) There may be challenges ahead, but they are nothing you can't handle because the Master is with you.

PREPARE TO SHIFT

Throughout this book I have used the word *shift*. To bring clarity and understanding, there are several definitions for the word *shift*. The one applicable to this chapter is defined as "to change, to change the position or alter, to move or remove from one place to another."[5]

A shift can also mean a change from old thoughts or habits and patterns of doing things that keep us from fulfilling the things God has called us to do. He desires for us to have a renewed mind where this is concerned. A mind in which we will change from the former (old) things to a new way of thinking.

A shift will not always be a physical move. Yet, in some instances, a physical move is crucial to being effective where the Master chooses to use you. Have you been called to feed the hungry or develop a school in a Third-World country? Are you called to use your gift of grace to lead as an administrator to build inner city housing for the disadvantaged? Do you have an assignment to welcome guests or new members with words of encouragement as they enter the front door of your sanctuary? Whatever the Master has called you to do, prepare to shift or move to fulfill your assignment with urgency.

To assist you with an understanding of how a shift can be effective, consider an individual who desires to transition from their current employment to pursue a new career in order to fulfill the purpose he or she was created to do. In the previous position, the individual never felt a sense of fulfillment, but they had thoughts such as "If I can just get through the day," or "There has to be more for me!"

Are you in a current position where you know there has to be more for you? If you are, then it may be time to consider a change.

As the individual in the illustration diligently sought a new career where their talents and gifts could grow, they found the right position. The excitement and satisfaction they experienced were unexplainable. The talents and gifts that were hidden and dormant came alive. Most importantly, the new employer began to experience new growth in his company from the new strategies suggested to them by the new team worker who stepped out and took the risk to use their talents along with their gifts of grace. It was evident that both individuals received a blessing.

This is similar to the marketplace, your sphere of influence, where you will touch, connect, and encourage others with your gift of grace, to enliven them with your passion of the Master's love, and show them that their purpose must be fulfilled.

The time has come to shift. To be successful, please consider these three key steps as you begin to move forward.

1. Release unproductive relationships. Jesus hung out with sinners as He shared spiritual truth with the world through parables and completed the assignment His Father had given Him. He knew the heart and intentions of the people, yet He was not distracted by the wickedness of mankind and continued to demonstrate love to everyone. However, He knew to let only a chosen few get close to Him. He surrounded Himself with twelve hand-picked disciples.

These men were not perfect, but they were the support Jesus needed while He walked this Earth. By allowing those men to be close, Jesus was able to mentor. After Jesus's death and resurrection, most of them became apostolic leaders within the church.

The importance of positive relationships is vital as you shift to accomplish what the Master has called you to do in this season. Let us observe the productive friendship of four young men who found a way to assist their friend to receive his healing. It is interesting to note that a young paralytic, who was lame and full of faith, knew that when Jesus returned to the town of Capernaum, he would be there. In his mind, he did not know and had not planned all the logistics, but he was determined to receive his healing. The story does not tell us how long the four friends had known each other, nevertheless, his friends caught the vision with the paralytic and assisted him in his healing. As a result of the crowd that gathered to hear the Master teach, there was no way to carry him through the door of the house. Therefore, his four friends who stood with him in faith "broke through the roof" and lowered his bed down through the roof where the Master was teaching. When the Master saw the faith of the young paralytic and his friends, he immediately was healed (Mark 2:3–4). Will your present relationships withstand the test of time as your gifts are being used to bless the kingdom of God? There may be situations you will need them to pray, encourage, and stand with you. There will be places you will go where they will be reluctant for you to travel. Remind them that you will need them more than ever to stand and intercede with you as you fulfill the purpose the Master has created you to do.

2. Release negative mind-sets. Begin to see yourself in the special way that the Master has created you. Wrong thinking is the key to defeat. You are more than a conqueror. The glow of His anointing will be with you as you build hope, empower others, and release your unlimited potential to serve. A shift will also require a new vocabulary of positive words spoken to and over you. Do not listen to or take part in unproductive conversations that foster words that tear you down and not build you up. Daily speak God's promises of who you are in Him and what you can have.

3. Saturate yourself in prayer. I'll talk more about the key of prayer in chapter ten. For now, I want you to know that prayer is a necessary part of your shift. It will alert you to any tactics the enemy may attempt to use which will distract you from accomplishing your mission. When you saturate or soak yourself in prayer, your attitude, mind-set, and vision will be changed. You will no longer stay in the infant prayer realm of, "Now I lay me down to sleep," but you will learn how to create an open portal from heaven that rains down strategies upon your spirit. Then you know when it's is time to shift, how to go about it, and how to defeat and conquer the enemy when he tries to stand in your way.

Begin to shift or move by faith. Faith unlocks the door where you can gain access to the things of the kingdom. After you have been equipped, trained, and released by the Master and receive the blessings from your spiritual leader, you can begin to move forward to fulfill your purpose. You will know the time to shift when you experience a tug or check in your spirit. Sometimes, the feeling will not leave until you obey or take action. The Master speaks or talks with us in different ways. Only you can discern His voice when He speaks to you. When you get the go ahead from the Master to move forward, He will be with you.

TIME FOR THE UNVEILING

It is time for you to be unveiled. When you are unveiled, it will reveal to others the character of the Master within you. It will remove the cloud of fear and doubt that oftentimes prevents an individual from establishing true intimacy with God and discovering the secret treasures He has on His heart for them. It causes them to see their true beauty within as they use their gifts of grace to build others' faith.

The word *unveil* is defined as "to reveal or to uncover."[6] Have you been hidden? Is it time for you to be revealed? You may ask, "How will I know that it is time for me to be unveiled, to step out to move out and do what God has called and gifted me to do?" The answer is only God who created you can give you the definite or exact time for your unveiling. If He knows the number of hairs on your head and has ordered your steps, He will instruct and guide you to prepare for your unveiling.

Inner peace from the Master will also be a good indicator of your release and that it is time to unveil. Apostle Paul encourages the readers in Hebrews 10:36, "For you have need of endurance; so that after you have done the will of God, you may receive the promise." The promise you will receive is to fulfill all that God has for you.

Your spiritual leader, who the Master has also given insight, will acknowledge that it is time for you to go forth. They will have witnessed the confidence and enthusiasm you have demonstrated as you were trained and equipped and will be able to help you discern when you are to be released. They will witness the Christian maturity and growth you exhibit as you walked with your brothers and sisters who were in the infant state of discovering their gifts of grace.

There is a season and timing for the plans God has for us to be birthed. A season has a beginning when the individual is in preparation; the middle when they are continually learning, shaping, and exploring their gift to ensure as they near the end they are confident and competent of how they should move and flow. The end of a season is the culmination of preparation, learning, shaping, and exploring your gift with the confidence of knowing the time of release is here. During that time will come the phases of preparation, birthing, equipping, training, and then activation or releasing, also known as the time to unveil.

In the season of preparation or birthing, activation will not occur. There has to be a season of growth to learn and mature. This birthing will occur in stages as we are being equipped. This includes our gifts of grace.

It is important that the believer knows what the time of unveiling or being "uncovered, revealed, and sent forth" in your gift or call looks like. There was a season of time you prepared, now you are equipped, activated (mobilized), and released by God and blessed by your pastor to go forth and fulfill God's plans for you. Most importantly, you carry the peace and the anointing of God! Your plans may not necessarily be to depart from your church. There are many ministry needs inside the walls of the church to assist the body of Christ using your gift of grace.

You may also be called to fulfill an assignment outside your church, leaving with the blessing from God and your pastor. Or, you may receive the release of God to depart completely to fulfill the call to pastor or to assist a ministry in another region. Seek God to give you someone who will provide you with godly counsel and act as a spiritual father or mother to cover you in prayer as you move forward.

Now you are ready to be released. When your gifts are unveiled, they should be celebrated, not tolerated. Celebrating a person's gifts doesn't mean balloons are released into the sky and someone shouts from the housetops. It doesn't even mean someone will congratulate them.

To celebrate your gifts means you are in a place where your gift will be recognized and released to be used in the body of Christ and in the marketplace. Never forget that you have access to the Creator, our source of "Son light" and the One who desires us to be and accomplish all we can on Earth, which is a mirror of God's purpose in heaven.

MY MISSION OR MINISTRY ASSIGNMENT

Natural talent: Leadership, Organization, Writing
Gift of grace: Leadership, Exhortation, Prophesy

Since 1997, I have had the honor of serving and mentoring men, women, and youth through many platforms. I have led workshops for personal and spiritual development, helped people identify and walk in their gifts of grace, been involved in youth empowerment opportunities, and participated in gatherings and humanitarian efforts, just to name a few. Through these platforms, I have seen many individuals catch and embrace the vision God had for them. Recognizing their purpose in this earth was life-changing for them.

Some were blessed to achieve their dreams and pursue careers that used their natural talents, becoming lawyers, educators, bankers, social workers, and so on. Others discovered their gift of grace through the revelation of the Holy Spirit and chose to develop that gift by attending workshops my team and I conducted. Through the prompting of the Holy Spirit, individuals have furthered their studies to become ministers of the gospel, work in missions, coordinate a youth ministry, and fulfill other roles in ministry.

It is not my intent to tell you when it is time for you to shift or change your position, or when you will be promoted, elevated, or be activated in ministry. That is something only the Holy Spirit will do. Your responsibility is to be willing to heed His voice and obey His call. However, while it is God's role to tell you when to change positions, may I encourage you to step out and accept the challenge to become all that God has created you to be? He is counting on you to partner with Him to advance His kingdom. Is it time to move forward to walk out your prophetic destiny?

In part 2 of this book, I will share seven keys that will help prepare you for an unforgettable journey to places in Him you have never been yet desired to go. To reach these places in God, you will have to embrace change so you will shift and move forward in your gifts and callings. Read on to discover how to access all that the Master has for you.

QUESTIONS FOR PERSONAL OR GROUP REFLECTION

1. What stage do you believe you are in: discovering your gifts, remaining hidden in the house, or poised to be unveiled and begin to move into all He has for you?

2. What has the Holy Spirit been speaking to you as you were reading this chapter? Is there something He's calling you to step out and do?

3. How would you describe your "marketplace"? In what ways can you use your gifts in that sphere?

MEDITATION FOR TRANSFORMATION

Your seat of destiny or your special or unique place of ministry plays a role in your vocation or career. In some workplaces, we have to use caution and be watchful in how we share our faith due to ethical standards or workplace restrictions. With this in mind, has there been a time you have shared or would like to share your faith and use your gift to encourage and bless your colleagues? How are you able to do it in a way that respects the culture of the company you work for? Use Galatians 5:22–23 and 1 Timothy 2:1–2 to help guide your answer.

YOUR GRACE IN ACTION

Write one idea that you would like to develop as a project to help others fulfill their purpose and live a meaningful life. What steps will you take to complete this project?

PRAYER OF PARTNERSHIP

Heavenly Father, I thank You for being my Creator and for giving me "Son light." As Psalm 139:14–16 says, "I praise you because I am fearfully and wonderfully made; your works are wonderful, I know that full well. My frame was not hidden from you when I was made in the secret place, when I was woven together in the depths of the earth. Your eyes saw my unformed body; all the days ordained for me were written in your book before one of them came to be" (NIV). You know the desires of my heart and will help me to fulfill all that You have for me. When I stumble, You will stretch out Your hand to lift me up before I fall. And You will open doors of opportunity that man has said were shut for me. In Jesus's name, amen.

PART II

BUILDING YOUR
SPIRITUAL TOOLBOX

ONE DAY A friend shared with me a story that relates a spiritual truth we can apply to our lives. Although the circumstances are not real, I was moved by the account and wish to share it with you. I pray that you will embrace these truths as you move to change your position.

An elderly grandfather presented his grandson with a small, old, rusty toolbox as a gift upon his high school graduation. The grandson graciously received the gift, though his mind was filled with concerns about money for college. His father died when he was five years old, and there never seemed to be enough money for his mom, little sister, and himself. His academic performance in high school was good, but it wasn't enough to earn him a scholarship that would cover all of his expenses for four years of college.

The grandfather asked the young man not to open the small, rusty toolbox until the end of the first semester of his freshman year in college. He agreed, and thanked and hugged his grandfather for his kindness. His grandfather gave him the key to the toolbox, and the young man placed it on his key ring.

At the end of his first semester in college, the young man traveled home and remembered the toolbox hidden in the closet of his room. His grandfather had passed away while he was in college, but the young man was unable to attend his funeral. He was happy to remember the good times he and his grandfather had together.

When the young man walked to the front door of his home, tears welled in his eyes. As he entered, he greeted his mom with a big hug, caught up on the latest news, and then went to his bedroom. He removed the key from his key ring, walked swiftly to the closet, and found the toolbox tucked away in the back. He pulled out the rusty, old box and took it to his desk, where he inserted the key. He turned the key in the lock and the latch popped open. Raising the lid slowly, he looked inside and found rusty old tools.

He opened his desk and pulled an old, tattered cloth out of the top drawer. Lifting each tool out one by one, he wiped them off, thinking back on the projects he and his grandfather worked on together.

When he lifted out the last tool, he noticed a white envelope lying on the bottom. He was puzzled. He took the envelope and began to open it with unsteady hands. Inside the envelope was a letter along with another key. This one was a tiny, shining gold key. Holding the key in his hand, he removed the letter from the envelope and began to read the words his grandfather wrote to him.

"Hello, grandson! I am so very proud of you and all that you have achieved in school. I wanted to see you one more time to let you know how much I loved you, but it was not meant to be. My appointed time had come. I had completed what I was destined to do in the earth. This is your time! I know you did well your first year in college and will do very well in your vocation in life. Your dad and I taught you many things. Do not forget them. You have a natural ability to build things, as well as a precious gift of leadership. Cherish and protect them both.

"There are seven spiritual truths that I leave with you as my legacy on behalf of your dad and me. Please accept and take them wherever you go. The Master has need of you and desires for you to fulfill your purpose in this earth. The best is yet to come, grandson.

"Oh, I forgot the small, shining gold key in the envelope. The key symbolizes the seven spiritual truths, or life nuggets, to always remember as you complete your education, begin your career, and grow in life. These truths will take you farther than you have wanted to go and cause you to experience things you never thought you would. I pray God's blessings on the beautiful and prosperous life you will live.

"Your grandfather."[1]

In the remaining chapters, I will share seven keys that will help you position yourself for change so you can successfully shift, move forward in your gifts, and fulfill the purpose God has birthed within you.

Chapter Eight

THE KEY OF WISDOM

THE YOUNG MAN sat quietly in the receptionist's area, waiting to be called for an interview. A new graduate from a local technical school, he was excited about the opportunity to interview for a lead teacher job in a new technical school. Suddenly, he heard his name. "Mr. Andrew, please enter the second door to your right. Mr. Clark is ready for your interview."

During the interview, he felt excited and confident in his responses to Mr. Clark's questions. He knew he could be a great asset to the company and shared some of the many creative strategies he wanted to implement if given the chance. At the conclusion of the interview, Mr. Clark thanked the young man and informed him that other candidates were being considered. He said he would be contacted should they need additional information before making their final selection.

"I'm sorry, Mr. Clark, but I do not understand," the young man said. "The advertisement read that an individual with advanced skills in robotics was needed to fill a high-tech teaching job. I meet all the qualifications."

Mr. Clark explained again that there were other applicants they needed to consider before making a decision. Upon hearing his reply, the young man quietly muttered, "Another rejection." before standing up, shaking hands with his interviewer, and walking away.

The young man was devastated. He had worked hard to prepare for the interview, but he felt in his heart that he was not chosen for the position. Sadly, the young man's hunch was correct. The job posting stipulated that the potential applicant needed to be a college graduate and have approximately five years of experience. The young man had a degree from a technical college, and this would have been his first job in his field.

This story illustrates the importance of the first key for moving forward to fulfill your assignment. That key is called *wisdom*. This six-letter word can be challenging to understand and difficult to define.

The word *wisdom* has a range of definitions, but the one that would apply to the young man's story is "the ability to make sensible decisions and judgment based upon personal knowledge and experience."[1] How, then, do we learn to make sensible decisions and have good judgment?

In their book *Gathering Wisdom*, the four co-authors make a profound statement: "Wisdom can be gathered. Wisdom can be learned, or gained. Wisdom cannot be taught."[2] If that is the case, then as Job asked, "From where then does wisdom come? And where is the place of understanding?" (Job 28:20). The answer is found just a few verses later: "God understands its way, and He knows its place" (Job 28:23).

In these verses, Job made it clear that only the Master, who created wisdom, knows how to obtain it. The authors of *Gathering Wisdom* came to the same conclusion; they wrote that because wisdom cannot be taught, the number one source for gaining wisdom is the Master Himself. Proverbs 2:6 says, "For the LORD gives wisdom; from His mouth come knowledge and understanding." He imparts wisdom by allowing us to grow through life experiences, which are the best teacher.

THE WORD OF GOD IS WISDOM

Did you know that God's Word will give you understanding about a situation you have been struggling with for a long time? Solomon says, "So that you incline [bend down] your ear and [diligently] apply your heart to understanding" (Prov. 2:2).

Gloria Copeland wrote in her book *And Jesus Healed Them All* that we should incline our ears to hear the Lord's sayings. She wrote, "Desire and go after God's Word. Put your ear in position to hear the word of faith preached. Don't wait for someone to come to your town. Go to where the Word is being preached."[3] When we earnestly embrace and hold on to His Word, the "light" of discernment will be illuminated within us and God will reveal which way or how we should move.

THE VALUE AND REWARD OF WISDOM

The process of mining for silver or gold is rigorous. Oftentimes it takes months to discover a piece large enough to have some value. When the persistent person uncovers a nugget of worth, they will cherish that moment of success for a lifetime.

The pursuit of wisdom should be the same. We should persistently seek those nuggets of gold and cherish each one once found. We do this by not making decisions without seeking God and inclining our ears to hear what is on His heart in this season. As Solomon wrote, "If you... search for her [wisdom] as for hidden treasures; then you will understand the fear [reverence] of the Lord, and find the knowledge of God. For the Lord gives wisdom" (Prov. 2:4–6).

When facing challenging situations, do not be perplexed. Proverbs 2:3 says that "if you cry out for insight, and lift up your voice for understanding" (AMP), it will manifest. If you lack direction, engage in earnest prayer. Seek and cry out to God to show you what to do or how to handle a particular situation. He has promised to answer. James 1:5 says, "If any of you lacks wisdom [to guide him through a decision or circumstance], he is to ask of [our benevolent] God, who gives to everyone generously and without rebuke or blame, and it will be given to him" (AMP).

I am reminded of the parable in Luke 11:5–8 of the man who received a knock on his door at midnight. A friend was at the door asking for three loaves of bread to feed another friend who had come to visit. But the man did not open the door. Instead, he said, "Do not bother me; the door has already been shut and my children and I are in bed; I cannot get up and give you anything" (AMP).

The friend continued to knock until the man gave him the bread he needed. Can you imagine what would happen if we would be persistent to incline our ears and apply our hearts to wisdom (Prov. 2:2). If we would do as this proverb instructs, our lives would be enriched with the principles and skills needed in every personal, business, and spiritual transaction.

Remember the words of King Solomon, "Wisdom is the principal thing; therefore get wisdom. And in all your getting, get understanding" (Prov. 4:7).

QUESTIONS FOR PERSONAL AND GROUP REFLECTION

1. King Solomon writes about the value of wisdom in Proverbs 2:4, "If you seek her as silver, and search for her as for hidden treasures..." Share what this verse means to you.

2. The four coauthors of the book *Gathering Wisdom: How to Acquire Wisdom from Others While Developing Your Own*, write that wisdom "cannot be taught, but must be gained through experiences."[4]

Describe a situation you faced in life that helped prepare you for something God had for you in the future?

3. Have you shared this experience with others, perhaps someone learning how to be successful in life? If so, how did the person respond?

MEDITATION FOR TRANSFORMATION

Did the young man mentioned at the beginning of this chapter use wisdom when he applied for the job? If not, why? If you knew this young man, how would you encourage or instruct him so he could be better prepared for the next interview?

YOUR GRACE IN ACTION

Reflect on a time in your life when you misinterpreted information or did not fully understand a topic and, as a result, lost an opportunity that would have led to greater advancement. Do you still carry the wounds? Share your experience.

PRAYER OF PARTNERSHIP

Thank You, Jesus, for the key of wisdom that You have freely given to me. With Your grace, I can be victorious in life. In Jesus's name, amen.

Chapter Nine

THE KEY OF PRAYER

THE SECOND KEY to embrace and carry with you is prayer. Abraham Lincoln, the sixteenth president of the United States, once said, "I have been driven many times to my knees, by the overwhelming conviction [firm belief] that I had nowhere else to go. My own wisdom and that of all about me seemed insufficient for that day."[1]

Imagine the sixteenth president acknowledging that he didn't know what to do and recognizing that his ability alone was not enough. Have you ever felt helpless or like giving up when you've tried all you knew to do? When you come to the end of yourself, it's time to seek God.

I want to share what happened when three people from Scripture were backed against the wall and had no option but to pray.

JEREMIAH—PRAYED TO PASS HIS ASSIGNMENT TO ANOTHER

A young lad name Jeremiah was called to a responsibility that he knew in his own power he could not fulfill. He was reluctant to accept the call, which was that he had been birthed from his mother's womb to be a prophet to the nations. (See Jeremiah 1:5; his calling was one of the fivefold ministry gifts.)

Sometimes youth feel ill-equipped or unprepared to accept

a charge or a leadership role that has been placed before them, and this was the case with Jeremiah. Yet regardless of how a person feels, they can be assured that the One who chose them—the Master—put the gifts, talents, and abilities within them to fulfill the call He placed on their lives, and He will guide them.

Many times, Jeremiah cried out in prayer to have the mantle passed to another. However, the Master reassured him with these words found in Jeremiah 29:11, "'For I know the plans and thoughts that I have for you,' says the LORD, 'plans for peace and well-being and not for disaster, to give you a future and a hope'" (AMP). Jeremiah was not received by everyone during his lifetime. But he didn't let that keep him from fulfilling his calling because through prayer he knew the mission was greater than people's opinions of him. (See, for example, Jeremiah 20.)

HANNAH—THE WOMAN WHO WAS CHILDLESS

In 1 Samuel, we meet a woman who experienced helplessness and possibly rejection in her situation, yet received strength and ultimately the answer needed through prayer. Her name was Hannah. She was childless, and her hope of one day becoming a mother seemed impossible. One day, driven with distress, she went to the temple to seek help. The Bible says, "She was in bitterness of soul, and prayed to the LORD and wept in anguish" (1 Sam. 1:10). Have you ever felt like Hannah did? Have you been in so much distress you were unable to even share with your family the deep pain within your heart?

Hannah made a vow to the Lord and said, "O LORD of hosts, if You will indeed look on the affliction of Your maidservant and remember me, and not forget Your maidservant, but will give Your maidservant a male child, then I will give him to the LORD all the days of his life, and no razor shall come upon his head" (1 Sam. 1:11). The words were spoken in her heart, not from her lips. So when Eli the priest saw her praying, he was puzzled, because her lips moved yet no sound was heard.

Thinking Hannah was drunk, the priest approached her and rebuked her. She replied, "No, my lord, I am a woman of sorrowful spirit. I have drunk neither wine nor intoxicating drink, but have poured out my soul before the LORD." (1 Sam. 1:15). The priest answered, "Go in peace, and the God of Israel grant your petition which you have asked of Him" (1 Sam. 1:17).

God answered her prayer, and she gave birth to a child she named Samuel. When Samuel was weaned, Hannah did as promised and dedicated him to the Lord. In doing so, she fulfilled the assignment God gave her. And the Lord blessed her with five more children (1 Sam. 2:21).

DANIEL—THE YOUTH WHO PRAYED

From a young age, Daniel knew his God, Jehovah, intimately through the power of prayer and by the miracles He performed in his life. Each test that was presented to Daniel by the king his God stepped in and delivered him.

As a teenager, he was taken into captivity when the Babylonians besieged Jerusalem. Nebuchadnezzar, the king of Babylon, instructed his head official to find four young Israelite men "in whom there was no blemish, but good-looking, gifted in all wisdom, possessing knowledge and quick to understand, who had ability to serve in the king's palace, and whom they might teach the language and literature of the Chaldeans" (Dan. 1:4).

The king's goal was to train Daniel and the others for three years, after which they would be prepared to enter the king's service. This scenario is similar to the men and women today who join the armed forces and are required to receive proper training before going into battle or acquiring a promotion.

As part of the king's training, the young men were to be fed the most delectable food and wine. However, Daniel, was determined that he would not dishonor his God, his people, or himself by eating the king's food or drinking his wine. He made a request to the overseer to be allowed to only eat vegetables and drink water for ten days (Dan. 1:12). After the ten days were over, the king examined Daniel and his friends. Their features were healthier and more robust, and the king acknowledged that they were ten times wiser than the ones who ate the king's food (Dan. 1:20).

Daniel was furthered tested when King Nebuchadnezzar had a dream that caused him much disturbance. He called for his men to interpret the dream. To no avail, none could interpret. The king was angry and made a decree that all those who could not interpret his dream would be put to death. So, he began to kill the wise men of Babylon. Daniel prayed again, and God gave him the interpretation for the king. Although, the king promoted Daniel, Daniel kept confident through prayer that he would honor only his God, Jehovah.

Another test proved that his God was with him as he sought him in prayer was when the king made an image of gold and placed it in the province of Babylon for all to worship. The king sent forth a call that all his leadership join together and stand before the gold image. A messenger shouted for all the people to fall down and worship this idol when they heard the sound of music. Those who do not obey would be thrown into the fiery furnace (Dan. 3:1–6).

Daniel was confident through prayer that the Master was with him and disobeyed the king's request. He and his friends were bound and thrown into the furnace, where the fire had been heated seven more times than normal. The men that bound them were immediately burnt up. However, as the king looked into the furnace, he was astonished as he saw four men walking around in the fire, not harmed, and the fourth was Jehovah (Dan. 3:19–25).

Have you experienced a fiery furnace moment as you stepped out to fulfill your call? When Daniel left his homeland and was thrust into captivity, he carried the power of prayer. He knew that his assignment would not be successful without prayer.

This challenge reminded me of the words of Oswald Chambers, "We have to pray with our eyes on God, not on the difficulties."[2] When we put our eyes on God, we'll be reminded of how big He is when compared to our problems. Prayer is powerful.

MEANS OF COMMUNICATION

There are various ways to communicate today. Cell and home (landline) phones, FaceTime, and Skype are just a few communication tools that effectively transmit messages.

Prayer is the tool we use to communicate with God, and it is vital to having a successful and purpose-filled life. Unfortunately, this is the least-used tool in many believers' spiritual backpacks. A two-way conversation is a must. Communicating with God will release the answers we have been waiting to receive. The Master will give us strategies for moving forward and doing the things God has called us to do.

The Master desires to talk with you, and He wants you to be prepared to listen. Did you ever have a close friend in school with whom you shared your deepest thoughts or your dreams for your future? The Master desires for you to communicate with Him in much the same way and share your heart with Him.

PURPOSES AND PRINCIPLES FOR PRAYER

There are many principles that guide individuals in prayer. I would like to share five practical insights about this power source called prayer, so you can apply it daily and move forward to fulfill your purpose.

1. Prayer acknowledges our need for God.

When we pray, we as humans are acknowledging our need for God. We are recognizing Him as the source of all that exists. Acts 17:28 says, "For in Him we live and move and exist [that is, in Him we actually have our being]" (AMP). For example, several times while writing this book, I stopped to acknowledge my need of the Master's help through prayer. I knew that I could not complete this book in my own strength, but I needed Him to empower me with the wisdom and guidance of how to write so that you, the reader, will be blessed as you move forward to fulfill your assignment.

I sensed the nudge to keep writing because one of his children was crying out to Him on what to do and how to move next with the plans outlined for their life. As a result, God was already behind the scene imparting to me how to write this book to launch you into your destiny. Ultimately, the Master is the only One who can do anything about our problems or supply the answer. The power of prayer is life-changing.

2. Prayer is something we learn by doing.

How does one learn to pray? E. M. Bounds, a gifted author on prayer, once said, "Prayer is not learned in the classroom but in the closet."[3]

You may remember learning to ride a bicycle as a child. You had to practice until you could ride by yourself. This is similar to how we learn to pray. Some will find prayer easy while others will find it challenging. Yet no matter which group you fall in, the more you practice, the better you become. The more you communicate with the Master, the easier you will find it to talk to Him and Him with you.

When you were first learning to ride your bicycle, you probably used training wheels to gain confidence that you could remain on the bicycle. After you rode your bicycle with the training wheels for a period of time, you were ready to go to the next level and remove the training wheels. Prayer is much the same way. You gradually learn the importance of prayer until you make prayer a daily part of your lifestyle.

The Master delights in those times when you can withdraw from everything and enter into your secret place (personal place of prayer) and pray. Whether you sit, kneel, lay prostrate; whether you lift your hands or just quietly worship Him, the Master welcomes you to join Him. Prayer is one of the most effective ways to get His attention.

Many individuals use the Lord's Prayer as a pattern for prayer. (See Matthew 6:9–13.) It is one of the most cited prayers in the church and is known around the world. Over time we must begin to incorporate other needs to pray with more depth, but as we're growing it can serve as a good model for prayer.

For example, the Lord's Prayer begins, "Our Father, who art in heaven." This reminds us that God is our spiritual Father, and His home is in heaven. The word translated "father" in Matthew 6:9 is *patēr* (pat-ayr), which comes from a root word that means "nourisher" or "protector."[4] It is a term of endearment. Therefore, when we call God "Father," we are acknowledging that He is everything to us, that He provides and protects us daily. *Father* is just one of the many names used in the Bible that depicts God's character. And there is so much more to discover!

3. Prayer brings benefits.

Praying with a spirit of humility will put us in a position to receive an answer. Humility is meekness or sincerity before God. It is a realization that we cannot do anything in and of ourselves but must rely totally on God. The Master is a gentleman and will respond to our prayers with a yes, no, wait, or not yet. If you've been praying about something but have not received an answer, keep praying and expect your breakthrough.

One benefit of prayer is that it builds a relationship with the Master. You can talk with Him every day and share secrets with Him just as you would with your best friend. The time spent with Him daily will be rewarded with an intimacy that allows you to know His heart and the things He has prepared for you.

A second benefit of prayer is that it builds our confidence. Remember when you prayed for a small thing and He answered? God's response showed you that you are important to Him. The Master delights in having you come to Him, and He will give you the desires of your heart. (See Psalm 37:4.) When God answers your prayer, you gain an assurance that He does hear you and will answer. The answer may not come immediately, but He will respond with a yes, no, or not yet!

When you seek Him in prayer, the Master will reveal to you what you need to know: whether you should take a particular job, relocate to another city, how to move forward with the gift or call He has on your life, etc. Have you ever sensed a tug inside your spirit when you had a major decision to make? Did the tug make you feel peace or anxiety? The Master will give you a tug to warn you or to guide you in what you should do next. As Proverbs 3:6 says, "In all your ways know and acknowledge and recognize Him, and He will make your paths straight and smooth [removing obstacles that block your way]" (AMP).

4. Prayer should be a regular occurrence.

Prayer is a discipline. Just as we eat three or more set meals a day to nourish our physical bodies, we need also to set a regular time to pray to feed our spirit. I enjoy spending time worshipping the Master early in the morning. At that time of day, my mind is free of distractions, and the house is quiet. Others may be comfortable praying at night when the day has ended. Once things have settled down, they can sit quietly in His presence.

No matter how busy your schedule is, find time in your day to meet with God and pray. Share your concerns and questions with Him. Ask Him to help you at your workplace, at school, or in your daily activities, and to give you favor with your supervisor, teachers, or merchants. Whatever time you select for prayer, cherish the time. It is a privilege to have the freedom to pray.

5. Prayer should be done according to God's will.

As we develop a lifestyle of prayer, many assignments will be birthed and fulfilled through prayer. This is why the key of prayer is so significant; it helps us establish an intimate relationship with God.

One of my favorite scriptures is 1 John 5:14–15: "Now this is the confidence that we have in Him, that if we ask anything according to His will, He hears us. And if we know that He hears us, whatever we ask, we know that we have the petitions that we have asked of Him." We must pray in accordance with God's will. One means of doing this is by praying the Scriptures, which is a way to God's heart. When we pray the Scriptures back to the Master, we have affirmed His Word. And we are able to be more specific in our prayers.

James 4:3 admonishes us, "You ask and do not receive, because you ask amiss, that you may spend it on your pleasures." Examine your prayers to see if they are selfish. That happens sometimes; we pray selfish prayers—prayers of "me, me, me" or, "I want; I want; I want." Søren Kierkegaard, the Danish philosopher, author, and theologian, once said, "The function of prayer is not to influence God, but rather to change the nature of the one who prays."[5]

Prayer shouldn't be complicated. It can be as simple as saying, "Master, thank You for blessing my neighbor and postman today. May every need they have be met, and may they come to know You as their Lord. In Jesus's name, amen."

Find another believer who will stand with you and pray until you fulfill your purpose in this season. Remember, believe that God has done the work and the answer will come. No matter how bad the situation seems, the Master is greater.

QUESTIONS FOR PERSONAL AND GROUP REFLECTION

1. Can you remember a time when you called out to a family member or friend for help? Share your experience.

2. Have you ever cried out to your heavenly Father when you were in need? How did He respond? Was there a difference in how the family member or friend responded to your cry for help, then the heavenly father? Please describe the feeling you received?

3. Why is it important to pray according to the Master's will?

MEDITATION FOR TRANSFORMATION

At times, the Master appears to be quiet and you receive no immediate response or answer to your prayer request. While you continue to fulfill your gift and call, it is important to remember the words in 1 Thessalonians 5:17, which reads,

"Pray without ceasing." When we do not hear from Him, what does it mean to pray continually without stopping?

YOUR GRACE IN ACTION

On a sheet of paper, write a prayer request to your heavenly Father about a situation you need Him to answer. Place the sheet in an envelope, date it, and put it in a safe place for approximately thirty days. Continue to pray and expect God to answer the prayer. At the end of thirty days, remove the envelope from its safe place, open it, and write about the experience in waiting on God and your expectations.

PRAYER OF PARTNERSHIP

Thank You, Jesus, for giving me the privilege and honor of seeking and knowing You through prayer. Amen.

Chapter Ten

THE KEY OF FAITH

Dr. Ben Carson, author, politician, and world-renowned neurosurgeon, demonstrated great faith as he accepted the assignment to "successfully separated two seven month-old conjoined twins who were joined at the head."[1] With a team of doctors and twenty-two hours later, the miracle had been performed by the doctor who stepped forward through the eyes of faith to see both babies live and have their own lives.[2]

Dr. Carson said "Great things were going to happen in my life, and I had to do my part by preparing myself and being ready. I am a good neurosurgeon. That's not a boast but a way of acknowledging the innate ability God has given to me. Beginning with determination and using my gifted hands, I went on for training and sharpening my skills."[3]

The book *Gifted Hands* tells a personal story of the challenges Dr. Carson had to overcome as an adolescent to become the famed neurosurgeon. As a student, Dr. Carson battled with defeat, doubt and fear, poor academics, and more. His mother, a single mother with little education, worked tirelessly outside the home to provide the basics for him and his brother. However, his mother knew she was the catalyst to ignite hope within him and his brother to become young men of excellence. She embraced her faith and developed a disciplined homework plan for her sons. The homework discipline paid off. Ben excelled in his academics and his behavior improved.

Upon high school graduation, he was accepted to the University of Michigan Medical School, and further continued his education as he was accepted as a resident in neurosurgery at the John Hopkins Hospital in Baltimore, MD.[4] With the key of faith, Dr. Carson rose to the top of his career. He has received many awards and achievements for His outstanding work. His mother's faith was contagious as Dr. Carson has credited his own unshakeable faith for how his gifts were discovered, trained and refined, and then released to bring healing to so many lives.

FAITH—THE FIVE-LETTER WORD

Faith is a subject that has been deeply researched, yet it is often a mystery. The Greek word for *faith* is *pistis*, which means "firm persuasion," or "a conviction based upon hearing."[5] Faith is the one thing that pleases the Master, and it comes with a condition. One must trust and believe the Master, no matter how the situation or circumstance appears. What He says will come to pass.

Faith is not a theory. We cannot fathom what faith is with our limited mind-sets. Faith is not based on feeling or seeing. It is the simple belief that the Master will do what He promises.

YOUR FAVORITE CHAIR

I want to share a simple analogy that will further explain what faith is and how it operates. Do you have a quiet area in your home where you can be alone? Do you have a favorite chair there? Perhaps you read the newspaper, a devotional, or a favorite novel in that chair. The chair is an inanimate object. It cannot speak or tell you how it feels. It is not human. Yet the chair brings you comfort, joy, or satisfaction.

If you're like me, you don't inspect the chair every time you use it to make sure it will hold your weight. You don't question the stability of the chair but are confident that it will be fine if you sit down.

Of course, God is not a chair. Yet do you believe He will take care of your future? Just as we believe our favorite chair will hold us, God desires that we have trust and confidence in Him. He knows what is best and will guide us to make healthy decisions as we move forward with purpose.

OPPONENTS OF FAITH

In anything we do, there will be opposition. Opposition is a part of life. Nevertheless, we can be assured that the Master's plan for our lives has already been worked out. Therefore, we have to move forward with faith and confidence that our end will be successful. Faith speaks yes, but doubt, disbelief, and fear say no!

Has the Master nudged you to move forward with your gifts and abilities but you're sitting and waiting for the entire plan to unfold? What holds you back: lack of finances, fear, uncertainty? As Martin Luther King Jr. once said, "You don't have to see the whole staircase, just take the first step."[6]

DISBELIEF AND FEAR

The two common opponents of faith are doubt and fear. Both have the same goal: to stop you from fulfilling your destiny. According to Dictionary.com, *doubt* means disbelief, fear, lack of confidence, and hesitation. The word *fear* means anxiety, doubt, despair, and worry. The Greek word translated "fear" is *phobos*, which is where we get the word *phobia*. *Phobos* means "fear, dread, terror"; it comes from a word that means "(to be put in fear); alarm or fright:—be afraid, exceedingly, fear, terror."[7]

Many times in the Bible, God said, "Fear not!" If we fear, we do not trust our spiritual Father to keep His Word or take care of our situation. Have you received an eviction notice or a pink slip signaling a job layoff? The Master is sovereign. He knew that would happen before it came to pass. He has a plan to fulfill in your life, and even when the unexpected happens, He has the situation under control. Trust Him. As Ralph Waldo Emerson once said, "All I have seen teaches me to trust the Creator for all I have not seen."[8] Having faith is key to moving toward your destiny.

OUR MODEL OF FAITH

During this journey called life, there have been those we have admired and possibly called our role models. Many times, adolescents, teens and young adults search to find role models to emulate. They delight in purchasing clothes, shoes, jewelry, and other paraphernalia to wear in hopes of becoming like them one day. Whether they are musicians, celebrities, sports players, coaches, or even a favorite teacher they hold with high regard, a role model can be important in a person's life. Besides parents, grandparents, and guardians who may often be regarded as role models, some of which are shining examples, others are disappointing as their actions fall short of those we would wish to call our heroes of faith, they still make an impact in our lives.

The word *model* is defined as "anything which serves, or may serve, as an example for imitation."[9] *Imitation* means "a person or thing that is not genuine or real."[10] As we continue to walk in our assignment, it is vital to have role models who are healthy examples. In today's world, there will be individuals who will attempt to divert you from moving in the purpose you were created to fulfill.

Jesus is our model or example of faith. He's not abstract or someone whose image we place on the shelf as an artifact or object. He is alive and desires you to trust Him to guide you with your plans. You will never be disappointed as you seek Him to carry out the promises He has for your life. He has an attentive ear and will listen when you call to Him. When we observe His life noted throughout the Scriptures, we will see that He left a pattern for us to succeed, to be prosperous, and to be a blessing to others. Let Him be your model of faith.

QUESTIONS FOR PERSONAL AND GROUP REFLECTION

1. Have you been in a situation in which you struggled with your faith? If the story is not too sensitive, please share your experience.

2. In the simple analogy of the chair, one sits down with the firm belief that the chair will hold their frame. Yet, as individuals, we are often challenged with anxiety and think things such as, "My bills are due, and I have no money." Or, "Why does this faith message seem so difficult to grasp and apply to daily life?" Do you have faith that God will "hold" you like the chair you sit in? Why or why not? Write your thoughts or share them with someone.

3. Have you ever had a role model? Share your thoughts or experience about the experience? Were you disappointed in something they did or the way they acted? Describe your feelings as God being your role model of faith as you step out and fulfill the plans He has for you?

MEDITATION FOR TRANSFORMATION

The action word *faith* may seem complex for many, but the Master has made it simple. He said to believe and with Him anything would be possible. (See Matthew 19:23.) What is one situation that you wish to see changed in your life to move forward and fulfill your purpose? Will you step out through the eyes of this simple word, faith, and believe it has been done?

YOUR GRACE IN ACTION

Have you ever found yourself or your family in a situation that appeared hopeless? It can be hard to trust God in the midst of a crisis. It can be hard to walk by faith and not by sight. (See 2 Corinthians 5:7.)

In his book *He Still Moves Stones*, Max Lucado said, "Faith is not the belief that God will do what you want. It is the belief that God will do what is right."[11] I'll add to that something Corrie ten Boom, author of *The Hiding Place*, once said, "Never be afraid to trust an unknown future to a known God."[12]

Take a moment to reflect on the goodness of the Master and how He brought you through difficult situations. If it is painful to think about, be still before Him and let His peace embrace you.

PRAYER OF PARTNERSHIP

Thank You, Jesus, for being my model of faith. In every area of my life, teach me to trust You and fear not. Amen.

Chapter Eleven

THE KEY OF GOD'S WORD— YOUR COMPASS

SEVERAL YEARS AGO, I planned a trip to a conference and traveled by car. In preparation, I ordered a trip pack from a travel agency, which sent me the best and shortest route to my destination. On the day of departure, I grabbed my luggage, briefcase, and map, and headed out the door. Much to my dismay, after I had driven approximately five miles, I realized that none of the mile markers synced with the instructions on the map. It was evident that I either misinterpreted the directions or was given the wrong information.

Have you ever started a trip and soon became aware that you were headed the wrong way? You think, "I checked and rechecked the map prior to departure. What went wrong?"

In the Old Testament, an assignment was given to a young man named Joshua. He was commissioned to be the next leader (his gift of grace) of the Israelites. His mission was to guide the Israelites over the Jordan River into Canaan, the land of promise and hope. His predecessor, Moses, had died, and now it was time for Joshua to continue the journey and complete the task Moses started.

In any assignment, one must have directions and a purpose for the trip, or else it will be unproductive and unsuccessful. In Joshua's story, the Master had passed the mantle to him along with the compass—the instructions he needed to follow. God promised that the Israelites would experience good success and prosperity if they followed the path He had set before them and not deviate from it. And He promises the same to you and me.

A COMPASS

A compass is defined as "a device for determining directions."[1] Although this device cannot guide us in making daily life decisions, this is the context in which I will use it in this chapter. Oftentimes, we seek directions in all the wrong places to help us fulfill the purpose the Master has birthed within us, when all we needed to do was consult the compass God gave us, which is His Word.

King David acknowledged that God has complete knowledge of His plans for us. He is aware of every area of our life and knows what is best for us, and what way and how we should go. He wrote in Psalm 139:3, "You chart the path ahead of me and tell me where to stop and rest. Every moment you know where I am" (TLB). Remember, to prevent unnecessary pitfalls, delays, and disappointments, we must follow the Master's instruction and not waver.

THE COMPANY HANDBOOK

Every new employee is given a manual with the company procedures. The policies are tailored for the employees who work at that designated company. The handbook may include job instructions and safety habits to follow within the facility and on the grounds. The handbook also may include company perks that would benefit the employee, such as vacation or sick time, levels of promotion, or paid tuition. Following the company manual will help the new employee transition smoothly into the job and perform their duties with excellence.

The Master has given us an instruction manual that will also provide us with guidance, much like the employee manual. This guidebook is the Bible, and in it God has given us promises.

Some promises are conditional, and others are unconditional. The conditional promises are those that require us to do something before the promise is fulfilled. For example, Proverbs 4:20–22 says, "My son, attend to my words; incline thine ear unto my sayings. Let them not depart from thine eyes; keep them in the midst of thine heart. For they are life unto those that find them, and health to all their flesh" (KJV). Life comes to those who attend to God's words.

In contrast, an unconditional promise has already been done. An example is found in Psalm 23:1, which is a favorite of many Bible scholars. David pens in this first verse, "The Lord is my shepherd; I shall not want" (KJV). He is encouraged that the Master will always take care of him and be his shepherd and protector.

The Bible, our compass through life, guides us into all truth (John 16:33) and affirms who we are. I am so glad to know that what the Master promised in Joshua 1:8 also applies to me. He said, "This Book of the Law shall not depart from your mouth, but you shall meditate in it day and night, that you may observe to do according to all that is written in it. For then you will make your way prosperous, and then you will have good success."

Theodore Roosevelt, the twenty-sixth US president, once said, "A thorough knowledge of the Bible is worth more than a college education."[2] Never leave home without your instruction manual, the Bible. It will take you to places in Him that you have never been but have desired to go. It's your compass for life.

QUESTIONS FOR PERSONAL
AND GROUP REFLECTION

1. Do you have a favorite promise in the Bible that you learned as a child and still recite today? Is it conditional or unconditional? What does this promise mean to you?

2. How can you use the Master's compass, the Bible, to find your way back to Him after a season of being disconnected?

3. In Psalm 139:3, King David wrote, "You chart the path ahead of me and tell me where to stop and rest. Every moment you know where I am" (TLB). King David illustrates here that God charts the path for him. Another meaning is God has navigated His plans for King David. What does this scripture mean to you and the plans God has for you?

MEDITATION FOR TRANSFORMATION

Mr. Roosevelt, the twenty-sixth US president, gave a profound quote in the last paragraph of this chapter. "A thorough knowledge of the Bible is worth more than a college education." Would you be willing to share your interpretation of this quote to a friend?

YOUR GRACE IN ACTION

Call a friend this week and extend an invitation to pray an encouraging prayer for them. Ask God to give you a promise from His Word to give them.

PRAYER OF PARTNERSHIP

Thank You, heavenly Father, for men of God, who carried the scribe anointing to write the Bible, which is my compass. Through this guide, I am given Your commandments, statutes, and promises to live by. Thank You for this gift. Amen.

Chapter Twelve

THE KEY OF ACCOUNTABILITY

Accountability is the fifth key that we need as we move forward to fulfill our purpose. It aligns with the Master's Word penned in Proverbs 11:14, "Where there is no counsel, the people fall; but in the multitude of counselors there is safety." In this chapter, we will examine the purpose of accountability and how it will prepare an individual to successfully fulfill their call in the earth.

THE PURPOSE OF ACCOUNTABILITY

The word *accountable* means "subject to the obligation to report, explain, or justify something; responsible; answerable."[1] The individual may even be held liable for the outcome. Stephen Covey, an educator and author of *The Seven Habits of Highly Effective People*, once said, "Accountability breeds responsibility."[2] I believe this is true. If accountability "breeds" responsibility, as Stephen Covey wrote, then it will develop our character. Character is what shapes our mind, body, soul, and spirit, which will determine the outcomes we experience.

Genesis 5:1 reads, "In the day that God created man, He made him in the likeness of God." If we were made and shaped after the image of God, there is nothing we can't do through Him. Therefore, we are driven to perform the work He has commissioned us to do in the earth.

There is one instance in the Bible that illustrates how when one individual did not assume accountability, tragedy occurred and ultimately the plans God had for them were not fully accomplished. A young man named David, who was noted in Acts 13:22 as a man after God's own heart and appointed king of Israel by the Prophet Samuel, was responsible to lead his soldiers in battle. Yet instead of fulfilling that duty, he sent Joab, his servants, and all Israel (the fighting men) on without him into battle while he remained at home (2 Sam. 11:1).

One may assume that he was possibly sick or needed to rest. After all, he was the king and was responsible to lead his men in battle. However, 2 Samuel 11:2 says, "Then it happened one evening that David arose from his bed and walked on the roof of the king's house. And from the roof he saw a woman bathing, and the woman was very beautiful to behold [look upon]." The Scripture does not say he was star gazing or praying on the roof. His mind had turned from his men in battle to possible covetousness.

I wonder if this situation would have ended differently had King David kept his mind on His original purpose. He had been given an assignment when he was commissioned to be king. This conquest was part of it, and it hadn't been accomplished yet. In the end, his men won the battle, but David was not directly part of the victory.

IS TRUST A LOST TRAIT TODAY?

Accountability also is a position of trust and is very significant in the Master's plans for your success. Proverbs 16:3 says, "Commit your actions to the LORD, and your plans will succeed" (NLT). The online Encarta English Dictionary defines *commit* as to "entrust something to somebody."[3] Solomon further adds in Proverbs 3:5, "Trust in the LORD with all your heart and lean not on your own understanding; in all your ways submit to him, and he will make your paths straight" (NIV).

Trust is an action word. As you prepare to move forward

with the plans the Master has for you, fear not. Have you ever been in the middle of an assignment and it seems overwhelming or there is to be no end in sight? You must allow neither outside influences nor distractions to get you off focus. If you stay the course and follow the plan, you will succeed.

In today's times, distractions will come to prevent you from having a clear and single focus. At that point, you must revisit your mission. Be accountable and responsible to complete what you have committed yourself to do.

LET THIS CUP PASS

In the Garden of Gethsemane, Jesus prayed, "Father, if it is Your will, take this cup away from Me; nevertheless not My will, but Yours, be done" (Luke 22:42). The cup was Jesus's crucifixion. His prayers that night were so intense that it appeared as sweat became as great drops of blood that fell to the ground (Luke 22:44). This is similar to the "coagulation formation of a mass of blood."[4] Even as He cried to His Father to release him from this assignment, Jesus knew it was His responsibility to complete this task. It was interesting to note in verse 43, that an angel was sent to strengthen Him to complete his assignment.

Is there an area of your assignment that seems challenging and that makes you feel like you can never complete it? Remember, the Master will not put more on you or ask more of you than you can do. He will send someone to strengthen and even walk alongside you. God has made a deposit in you to encourage and to release others to move or shift to fulfill their destiny. May I suggest that you prayerfully consider a mentor to assist or support you in fulfilling your goals or accomplishments? Be assured, this does not show a sign of frailty or an inability to accomplish the task. Rather, it is a sign of inner strength to acknowledge that you

need someone to walk alongside you and help you fulfill all
that God has called you forth to do.

THE ROLE OF A MENTOR

The word *mentor* can be defined as "a wise and trusted
counselor or teacher" or "an influential senior sponsor or
supporter."[5] A mentor is an advisor, coach, counselor, guide,
teacher, trainer, tutor, instructor, and more. Proverbs 15:22 is
a profound scripture that I have used to govern my life when
I need to make healthy life decisions that will bring success:
"Plans fail for lack of counsel, but with many advisers they
succeed" (NIV).

Sometimes we do not see the seed of greatness within us
that others see. All through my formative school years and
beyond, I can remember individuals who were important in
shaping my character and providing me with the guidance
to use my talents and abilities to grow. Interesting enough
as I sit and write this chapter, I am reminded of a teacher in
one of my elementary classes, who I will call, Ms. Bee.

One day she asked me to come to her desk. I walked fearfully with palms sweating past several rows of seats, feeling
the piercing stare of my classmates, until I reach the corner
of her desk. Much to my surprise, she said cheerfully, "Doris,
today you will lead the class out to the playground for recess."

"Me!"

"Yes," she said, "I have chosen you."

Due to my quiet manner, I was very seldom called upon
to participate. Why was I asked to perform this role that
seemed to be reserved only for the students who raised their
hands? What did she see in me?

Just imagine. Has anyone ever told you that you have a
special quality that is unique? From that day forward, the
experience with Ms. Bee still has a strong impact in my life
as I hear the words, "Lead the class out to the playground."

Everyone may not be a born leader, but we all can lead in our own way. Make a difference where you are and success will come if you stick with it long enough.

As I grew into a young adult, there was one individual who played a key role. This young man offered wisdom and at times would suggest that I participate in youth events to strengthen my talents. As the newly elected youth chairman of a large Christian organization, he began to search out youth for his leadership team who had a desire to excel and were willing to learn. Much to my surprise, he extended an opportunity to me along with several other youth to join. With the blessing of my parents and spiritual leader, I accepted the invitation. Under his tutelage, he gave us opportunities to grow.

I vividly remember one instance when he gave me the responsibility to develop my first workshop for an upcoming youth conference. Excited about this opportunity, I shared with the chairman the issues that youth are challenged with daily. I thought those points would be great for a workshop.

With his encouragement, I moved forward to gather a youth support team to assist with the planning process. Our goal was to assist youth to discover their purpose and how to make good life choices.

At the beginning of each planning session, ideas were shared, a few tears shed, and an atmosphere charged with energy as the youth began to see the workshop vision. A dramatic presentation called "Mirror, Mirror" became reality. They discussed the presentation with the chairman, who listened attentively and gave input where needed.

The presentation depicted eight characters who felt they were trapped in a web of self-defeat that prevented them from experiencing success. Ultimately, the key to their success came through discovering that it was not about the things they sought after but the inner qualities they possessed. In the end, the play was well attended with an overwhelming number of requests to present the workshop the next year.

Most importantly, it was noted by the chairman during the drama presentation, that several of the youths' talents ignited with promise as they performed their roles. One young man discovered he had a good speaking voice, which he never expected to receive a standing ovation during one of the scenes. Under the tutelage of the youth chairman, opportunities developed for him to use this gift, and he later became speaker for a youth retreat. Another youth, who assisted with cowriting the drama presentation, released her talent and later began a career in writing.

A mentor is important and can play a vital role in shaping our character for life. Have you ever been a mentor? Do you have a mentor? Age does not matter. Oftentimes, in the older years of our lives, we may need someone to strengthen, encourage, or speak into our lives that we still have more to do or give. Of course, we must use wisdom in selecting a mentor. Ask for help from mature advisors who will hold you accountable.

This youth chairman, Michael Shelby (bishop), gave so willingly of his time and wisdom, provided guidance, developed our strengths, and never discouraged the youth from stepping out to try new things that would help us become all that we could.

He has been the shepherd (pastor) of God's House for twenty-nine years, with his wife, Charlotte. God's House is located in Albuquerque, New Mexico, a thriving and growing multiethnic church that is active in the community and global outreach. Bishop Shelby is currently the assistant presiding prelate of New Destiny Fellowship where he oversees churches nationally and internationally.

Much of my success today has been due to those who have poured into my life, and gave me a platform to develop. I have been blessed to experience success in the call I have been sent forth and created to do.

The same is true in other professions. Many major

companies or organizations will assign mature executives to mentor young leaders to help them learn strategies for operating and leading a successful business.

QUALITIES OF A MENTOR

A good mentor can have a tremendous impact on a person's growth and success. Here are just a few characteristics to look for if a mentor is needed.

1. A mentor must be positive or affirming. Seek an individual or individuals who will celebrate your strengths and assist you with resources to strengthen your weaknesses. Ask them to be patient with you if you do not understand or comprehend information as quickly as they wish. Everyone learns differently and has the ability to succeed.

2. A mentor must be a visionary. A mentor who is a visionary sees the potential within the individual and finds strategies to cultivate those hidden wells of knowledge or ability to help them spring forth.

3. A mentor must be skilled. Pray and ask the Master to guide you to a skilled, well-trained individual who will assist you in further developing your talent or gift. A good mentor will not be intimidated by or jealous of your gifts but will rejoice to see the manifestation of God's purpose for your life.

4. A mentor must be dependable. With the world we live in being so fast-paced, seek individuals whose time will sync with yours. Do not place a demand on the individual that you or they cannot commit to. Refine your goals for the mentor relationship and how long you will need the individual's help. Ask

if they require a stipend for their time or if there is some way you can use your talents to assist them. For example, if the mentor has a community outreach program and is in need of someone to play the piano or sing, and you have those talents, offer to donate your services. Or if you have an organizational ability to coordinate food baskets to distribute to the elderly who are in need, you can offer them the use of that gift of grace. With this exchange of services, both of you will be blessed as you fulfill your call.

OBEDIENCE PLEASES THE HEART OF GOD

God uses pastors and ministries to teach us accountability. We are encouraged to honor and obey the leadership God has placed over us. Apostle Paul instructs us in Hebrew 13:17, "Obey those who rule over you, and be submissive, for they watch out for your souls, as those who must give account. Let them do so with joy and not with grief, for that would be unprofitable for you." When ministry is walked out biblically, these men and women keep us accountable and teach us to be responsible as we walk in our gifts. Remaining obedient to men and women like this pleases the heart of God.

Unfortunately and oftentimes, the word *obedience* is distorted, misused, and used to manipulate believers who seek to shift or move within or outside the walls to fulfill an assignment they have been called to do. We should never seek to walk in contrariness or have a spirit of pride. God hates both. This is disobedience. Our desire must be to please the Master in all that we say or do. Yet there are times when we will be drawn away from a ministry or an organization in order to complete a new assignment. Don't allow anyone to heap condemnation on you, but before making a major move, always seek the counsel of a designated leader or the individual to whom you are held accountable. If that leader is not aware of your gift or talent and your desire to be used, share how you feel. Be open and candid.

After you have talked with the leader about the call on your life and what God has put on your heart, if the leader believes the time is not right for your move, pause and pray.

A sincere leader has your spiritual well-being at heart. They are placed in the body of Christ not to prevent, hinder, or restrict you from moving. Moreover, a true leader of God has a heart to see each member develop and help them to fulfill their purpose in the earth. Accountability frees us up to use our gifts and accomplish all God has for us; it doesn't oppress.

QUESTIONS FOR PERSONAL AND GROUP REFLECTION

1. Accountability is significant to some and insignificant to others. Have you ever experienced the importance of accountability? If so, how has it helped you develop character?

2. What qualities would you look for when seeking a mentor? Why and how is a mentor important as we fulfill our purpose?

3. Is our obedience to leadership important to the heart of God, provided the leader walks in accordance to God's Word and His way? Please share your thoughts.

MEDITATION FOR TRANSFORMATION

If we examine the word *accountability*, it is a word that many have been challenged with in their Christian walk. He has left us His Word to obey and be held accountable. Our Master, is our role model, therefore, how would He respond to us in a court of law?

YOUR GRACE IN ACTION

For thirty days, would you be held accountable to read your Bible? Proverbs is a great book to read. It has thirty-one chapters; therefore, if you consent to read one chapter a day, you will have completed all chapters by the end of the month. Seek God for the month you should begin so you will be diligent to complete. Find a friend or someone you wish to be your accountability partner? Keep your journal and notepad close. God will speak amazing things to you. At the end of thirty days, write about your learning experience.

PRAYER OF PARTNERSHIP

Thank You, heavenly Father, for the key of accountability. Thank You for sending us godly men and women who help us to be accountable and teach us to be responsible as we walk out our purpose in the earth. Amen.

Chapter Thirteen

THE KEY OF PREPARATION

ALL OF THE seven keys are designed to help you prepare to fulfill your purpose, but the key of preparation is unique in that it is a call to be intentional about making ourselves ready for the Master's use. In every area of life, preparation is vital to success. To pass a driver's test, one must prepare. A master baker must rise early to prepare the bakery goods for his customers. When a mother or father faces an unexpected illness, all the family members must prepare to step up and assist to ensure the household functions smoothly. The same is true when it comes to moving in our gifts. Successful people are intentional about doing what is necessary to accomplish their assignment.

One of my favorite motivational speakers is Zig Ziglar. The author of *See You at the Top*, Ziglar once said, "You were born to win, but to be a winner, you must plan to win, prepare to win, and expect to win."[1] To be a winner who will succeed, you must prepare!

AWAKENING

In 2015, I was invited to a four-session workshop on the spiritual gifts. This was a great opportunity to increase my knowledge and insight about the gift of prophecy, learn the proper protocol for using this gift, and help others who may lack understanding about this gift that can transform an individual's life.

At the end of the training, the facilitator led us into an activation that allowed us to practice what we learned during the workshop. The class divided into groups of two or more according to instructions given, and the activity began. The individual who ministered to me began to pray that my faith would arise and be charged to receive all that God had for me. He spoke words of encouragement to my spirit.

Prior to attending the workshop, I had cried out to God, asking Him to guide me on how my ministry could be more effective and bless others in the kingdom. Little did the person ministering to me know that, as God spoke through him, a word was given that changed my spiritual direction. "My daughter, a little more preparation is needed!" were the essence of his words to me.

I was so intrigued with the word *preparation* that I began to cross reference it in several sources to find a definition that would bring clarity about what God was saying to me. One definition of preparation is "the action or process of making ready or being made ready for use or consideration."[2] A definition of the word *prepare* is "to make ready beforehand for some purpose, use, or activity."[3] The key concept in both definitions is to "make ready for use." In other words, additional steps may be needed to move forward to fulfill and possess your dream.

To illustrate, one young woman who desired to fulfill her dream was Amelia Earhart. She was the first woman to fly solo across the Atlantic Ocean. In her pursuit of this goal, she made ready and prepared herself through practice, perseverance, and persistence.

Another example is Lido Anthony "Lee" Iacocca. A former American automobile executive and author of *Where Have All the Leaders Gone*, Iacocca had a desire to fulfill an assignment that at the time seemed impossible. Yet, in the 1980s, he prepared to see his dream come to fruition, and it came to pass. He was instrumental in revitalizing the Chrysler Corporation.[4]

As I stepped out into new areas of leadership and means of using my gifts, I too had to apply the education and preparation I had acquired. I could not just stand there holding all that had been poured into me. I had to do something. With God as my guide, I had to make something happen. Of course, I was puzzled when I received the word about preparation from M. Leon Walters, but I was also excited. (Please note: He is the executive vice-president of Christian International Ministries Network (CIMN); and president, CI Central (CIC) and CI Family Worship Center (CIFWC).) It was evident that more spiritual growth and self-development were needed for me to be made ready for use. So, like Amelia Earhart, I began to prepare for my next move.

YOU CAN BEGIN AGAIN

Henry Ford, founder of the Ford Motor Company, once said, "Before everything else, getting ready is the secret to success."[5] How does one get ready?

First, re-evaluate the workshops you have attended, past or recent, to see if there was a common theme that drew you to do additional study to expand your skill or talent. Second, review your formal education to see if additional training is needed to enhance what you already know. Third, set personal and spiritual goals to accomplish the more that may be required. The natural goal might be to set a specific time of completion, and the spiritual goal might be to further your development through a Bible study course.

Last, find a place of worship, or an organization in the marketplace or the community, where you can practice your gift to build confidence to prepare for God to launch you forward. Again, seek accountability to ensure you are under protection in prayer as you move forward to do God's work.

With that in mind, I want to spend the rest of this chapter

sharing five life nuggets that will help you to prepare to use your gifts and fulfill your purpose.

Believe in yourself.

Norman Vincent Peale, renowned author of *The Power of Positive Thinking*, once said, "Believe in yourself! Have faith in your abilities! Without a humble but reasonable confidence in your own powers you cannot be successful or happy."[6]

Believe is a word noted throughout the Bible that tends to precede what the Master says we can have; all we need to do is embrace the small seed of faith within. Repeat out loud with me, "I have greatness inside of me."Do you feel excited that you were chosen to be and do great works through the Master? Now believe, then achieve and move forward.

Realize that you are what you think.

No matter what you think about yourself or what inadequacies or insufficiencies you believe you have, you are who the Master says you are. You can do all things through Christ who gives you strength (Phil. 4:13). What does this verse mean? It's saying that we can do nothing in and of ourselves. We need the Master, the Creator of all, to help us.

Set personal and spiritual goals.

Meeting goals or the process to achieving goals are important because they shape your character and give you more confidence that you will accomplish what has been set before you to do. Working toward becoming a better time manager may be an excellent goal to set to achieve as a personal objective. It takes discipline, however, to plan and complete each step to meet your goal and achieve what you seek to accomplish. When you set goals and discipline yourself to meet them, you will not be overwhelmed but will instead have confidence that your assignment will be completed on schedule.

Spiritual goals are markers that guide us in our spiritual growth. They help give us direction and gauge whether we are on track to make the progress we seek in life. A spiritual goal may be to spend more time in Bible study or prayer. Both will help you grow tremendously.

Take one step at a time.

This step does not call for immediate action, but do not lose momentum. You are running a marathon, not a 5k, so take one step at a time, stay focused, and keep the assignment in view. If you take one step at a time, eventually you'll be able to say, like the apostle Paul, "I have fought the good fight, I have finished the race, I have kept the faith" (2 Tim. 4:7).

Submit to and answer the call.

Now that you believe the Master has called you forth for your assignment and has prepared you to gain more confidence and understanding in the plan He has for you, set personal and spiritual goals. These may include enrolling in a class or attending a workshop that will increase your knowledge about your gift or talent. You are prepared to submit to the call, move forward, and fulfill your assignment.

Not everyone will feel the nudge from the Master to embrace the positive nuggets just presented. Yet you have been called for this season because you have great potential to accomplish all God has for you. Be obedient to the Master and do His will, and you will be abundantly blessed.

QUESTIONS FOR PERSONAL AND GROUP REFLECTION

1. Preparation may seem to be a daunting task, but it is essential to the success of your dream. What steps do you need to take in order to move forward? Are they realistic?

2. Do you believe you can do whatever the Master has presented to you? To believe means to accept that you can be successful in accomplishing whatever you are called to do.

3. Are you hesitant or fearful to step out and fulfill your purpose?

MEDITATION FOR TRANSFORMATION

What is one way you can begin to make yourself ready for use? It is not too late. Take one step at a time and you will experience positive results for your life.

YOUR GRACE IN ACTION

1. At the top of a sheet of paper in your journal or notepad, write *"My Assignment for the Kingdom of God."* Remember, the marketplace is part of the kingdom. Place the *date* directly under your assignment header.

2. If you have discovered and identified your gift of grace, write it directly under the date.

3. Define or write what your assignment is in one sentence. Here are a few examples.

   a. My assignment is or I have been gifted or called to teach in a third world country. As a suggestion, find someone who has worked in missions in another country and asked them to share their experience. It is not necessary to be overseas. There are places within the United States that need mission workers.

b. My assignment is or I have been gifted or called to work with an at-risk population of children in a foster or guardian home.

c. My assignment is or I have been gifted or called to assist a pastor, who is in need of volunteers to help him rebuild his church after a storm devastation.

d. My assignment is or I have been gifted or called to develop a nonprofit organization for humanitarian efforts.

The list is endless and unlimited to what God has for you. Ask yourself, will this be a long- or short-term assignment? Take into consideration your present employment, finances needed for an overseas trip, or to assist you for a period of time. A physical may be needed, passport, resume, and more to prepare for your ministry gift.

4. Write the word *preparation.*

a. Begin with prayer and ask God how He desires you to move forward with this gift or call.

b. Seek godly counsel from your senior leader or spiritual father/mother and share with them what God has given you and be attentive to what God is saying through them.

c. If you need to refresh your skills, update your ministry certificates, move forward and contact the various resources.

d. Pause and pray again. Wait for the next move from God to direct you.

PRAYER OF PARTNERSHIP

Thank You, Jesus, for giving me the talents, abilities, and spiritual gifts to be successful in life. Thank You for open doors and the opportunities You have created to help equip me to bless the body of Christ and the marketplace. Amen.

Chapter Fourteen

THE KEY OF TIMING

Timing is the last key you need to prepare to shift into or move forward in your assignment. We often say, "What happened to the time?" We each have twenty-four hours in a day and seven days in a week, yet we often are challenged with time. For example, the deadline was set and a promise given three days ago to deliver important paperwork to a friend. However, eight days have passed and the task still hasn't been completed. Being mindful of time in today's world is a great discipline many need to sharpen, not only for their personal lives but also to fulfill the Master's assignment.

I too am challenged with time, but I'm not referring to time management. Several years ago, I knew it was time to replace my worn, fifteen-year-old Chevy van. It was a faithful member of our family that had taken us to baseball and football games, track practices, family vacations, and more. The ultimate sacrifice for our aged van was the four years we used it to take our son to and from college out of state. We stuffed it again and again with all the items he would need for his dormitory, from his freshman through his senior years.

It was just a matter of time before it would stop running, but we did not have plans to purchase another van in the near future. My heart—and my budget—wanted to hold on to the van a little longer. However, safety needs and an increase in repairs seemed to cry out, "It's time!" As the

135

Bible says, "To everything there is a season, a time for every
purpose under heaven" (Eccles. 3:1).

For many of us, it is time to let go of things that are preventing us from moving forward. For some, that means
releasing material items that are no longer needed. For
others, it means releasing emotional baggage that keeps you
bound and closed to new horizons or paths.

CHRONOS TIME

There is more than one way of looking at time and God's
timing. There is chronological time, which in the Greek is
the word *chronos*. It means a "space of time"—the seconds,
minutes, and hours that make up a day.[1] *Chronos* time is
sequential. In our daily lives, we use clocks and watches to
monitor time. The establishment of fast-food restaurants in
the early 1900s was an indication of how mindful people were
becoming of time. Today, people are constantly looking for
new ways to maximize their time. In fact, Tracy V. Wilson,
author of the article "How Fast Food Works," says fast-food
restaurants have grown in popularity because they satisfy a
need for people who, more and more, lead a fast-paced life.[2]

More often than not, we focus on *chronos* time as we seek
to accomplish important tasks or achieve goals. Yet there is
another type of time that for many seems elusive or intan-
gible. It's called *kairos* time.

KAIROS TIME

Kairos time is a divine moment in time, "opportune or sea-
sonal time," "a fixed and definite time." It is the time when
something is fulfilled or manifested.[3] God has a set time for
you to step forth into your destiny. It is not fate, but a divine
moment. Remember, "He has made everything beautiful in
its time" (Eccles. 3:11).

A *KAIROS* MOMENT

In the Book of 2 Kings, there is a story that illustrates a kairos moment. I love this story because the awesomeness of God is seen throughout.

In 2 Kings 4:8–15, the prophet Elisha was travelling through the small village of Shumen, and a woman from the area saw him from a distance. She had just prepared a meal, and invited him to come and eat with her and her husband. Elisha accepted her invitation. She let him know that it was her honor to have him in her home. The Shunammite woman was a person of influence and had been noted for her hospitality (her gift of grace).

After that initial invitation, Elisha and his servant, Gehazi, often stopped by to visit this woman and her husband at their home during their travels to assist God's people. The woman was honored to assist this man of God and asked her husband if they could, according to some theological readings, build a room for him to stay in during his visits. Her husband agreed to build the room.

Elisha desired to return the kindness this woman had shown him. So one day during their visit, Elisha asked Gehazi what they could do for the woman. Gehazi replied, "She has no children and her husband is old!"

Elisha asked Gehazi to call the woman. As she stood waiting, Elisha said to her, "Because you have been good to us, we would like to do something special for you. This time next year, you shall embrace a child." The woman was overwhelmed and said, "Oh no, my Lord. Man of God, do not lie to your maidservant." The petition was granted as the prophet had spoken, and she had a son.

The Shunammite woman waited many years to have a child and it appeared hopeless, but God made her a mother in His divine *kairos* time. Never give up! What seems to be hopeless or out of control in your life can be a way the Master is working something out. Continue to hope and expect the situation to change according to His Word.

BE A GOOD STEWARD OF TIME

Many wait for the right time to come before they move into what the Master desires for them. Yes, we need to have a sense of knowing before we proceed to do anything. Yet many of us are still waiting for a sign or to hear from God when He has already given us the green light.

It is time to seek the Master's face. Begin to use the gifts of grace you have been given to usher in the presence of God within your home and place of worship. Prophetic voices are needed in the body of Christ today to restore what has been lost and proclaim that the Master is ready and willing to meet us at the appointed time and manifest His gifts to us.

How can we know when it is God's "opportune time" for you to pursue or walk in your assignment? Here are five guidelines to keep in mind.

1. Listen for the voice of God and guard your ear gate.

The ear is an important part of the body. It is designed to hear sound. The Master speaks to us in different ways: in our spirit, through His Word, and sometimes audibly. Have you ever heard the voice of God audibly? It's as if someone is standing or sitting close and speaking directly in your ear.

One day, I was driving in my car and lost my directions to my destination. Suddenly, I felt the ugly spirit of fear arise. I refused to accept the feeling and quietly asked God to help me find my way home. Suddenly, I heard a voice as loud as if someone was sitting in the passenger seat say, "Turn here!" I have heard God's voice before but never with such clarity. We have to be sensitive to hear the voice of God before we proceed to fulfill our assignment.

2. Submit to proper authority.

After you have sought the Lord through prayer, His Word, and godly counsel, you are clear to step out and move forward. This step is crucial as you shift. Oftentimes, an individual will shift out of a selfish desire and become impatient.[4]

To be under the covering of godly protection will prevent us from being disobedient. In Hebrews 13:17, Paul admonishes us to, "Obey those who rule over you, and be submissive for they watch out for your souls, as those who must give account. Let them do so with joy and not with grief, for that would be unprofitable for you." We must respect our leaders who walk according to God's way. When we step out and do our own thing without any regard to leadership, we are submitting to the flesh and therefore God is not pleased with our actions. God is supreme, yet He has placed godly leadership within the body to guide and watch over us.[5]

3. Serve with a clean heart.

Delight in the Master and serve Him with righteousness. You have been set apart for this time and season to do greater works for the kingdom. Remember, we must not walk in unforgiveness and bitterness. Release all that hinders you and walk freely in love.

4. Move forward with a spirit of humility.

The Scripture says, "The heart is deceitful above all things, and desperately wicked; Who can know it?" (Jer. 17:9). Walk in meekness and see the fulfillment of all the Master has for you. Meekness is one of the nine fruits of the Spirit. It demonstrates the beauty of God. It represents a spirit of humility. It does not display arrogance but demonstrates the love of God through our actions to others.

5. Combine prayer with fasting.

Prayer is the key to unlock the answer to your need. Sometimes we do not know how or what to do to move. If that's the case with you, stand still. Wait! The Master will answer.

When faced with a hard thing or a situation that seems impossible while you are on your assignment, combine prayer with fasting. Set your will to fast. Fasting is the companion to prayer. Isaiah 58:6 reminds us what fasting will do, "Is this not the fast that I have chosen: To loose the bonds of wickedness, to undo the heavy burdens, to let the oppressed go free, and that you break every yolk…" God will subdue your flesh and give you the peace of God until the answer comes. Try it! It will not cost you nothing but a healthy body, mind and spirit.

REDEEM THE TIME

Have you ever asked, "Can time be redeemed?" In the natural sense, *chronos* time cannot be redeemed. It is gone and can never be restored. It is not humanly possible to turn back time. But the Master controls time, and in 2 Kings 20:1–11, He did just that.

King Hezekiah became sick, and the prophet Isaiah told him to set his house in order because he was going to die (2 Kings 20:1, AMP). Hezekiah knew God and petitioned Him through prayer. He knew the Master was full of compassion and mercy. So Hezekiah reminded the Lord of His faithfulness and how he had walked before him with his whole heart and did what was right.

The Master heard Hezekiah's prayer! He sent the prophet Isaiah back to him to say, "I have heard your prayer, I have seen your tears. Behold, I am healing you; on the third day you shall go up to the house of the LORD. I will add fifteen years to your life and save you and this city [Jerusalem] from the hand of the king of Assyria; and I will protect this city for My own sake and for My servant David's sake" (2 Kings 20:5–6, AMP).

The sign given to indicate that Hezekiah would be completely healed was that the shadow of the sundial (indicating the time of day) would go back ten steps. (See 2 Kings 20:9–11, AMP.) Though it was humanly impossible for that to happen, God confirmed His word to Hezekiah!

The even better news is that *kairos* time can be redeemed. The word *redeem* is the Greek word *exagorazō*, which means "to make wise and sacred use of every opportunity for doing good" and "buying up the opportunity, a release."[6]

The Bible says God "is rich in mercy, because of His great love with which He loved us" (Eph. 2:4). When we come boldly to Him in faith and repent, He is merciful to forgive and restore us. Repent of any wasted time and ask God to extend His mercy and give you another opportunity to accomplish His desires for you. His grace is available to you.

THE SECRET IS OUT

God designed a master plan for your life the moment you were conceived, and God desires that you accomplish all He has for you in the earth. You have been a well-kept secret. This is the time to activate your gifts and talents for the kingdom of God and the marketplace. May your journey begin today!

QUESTION FOR PERSONAL AND GROUP REFLECTION

1. Do you believe God still performs miracles today? What miracles has God performed in your life? Please encourage someone who is in need of a miracle with your story—someone who is sick, feels hopeless, or is in despair.

2. How have you seen God's timing at work in your life? Write your definition of *chronos* and *kairos* time.

3. How does one redeem the time (or lost opportunity) that has passed? Has this happened to you? Are you willing to share this experience with a friend who understands and will assist you in continuing to pursue your purpose? Remember to trust God, who gives second chances.

MEDITATION FOR TRANSFORMATION

What "stuff" have you hung onto that has kept you from stepping out to embrace the new? Give an example of a new idea, new venture, new journey, new job, or new location that you have desired to pursue but were reluctant to take action on.

YOUR GRACE IN ACTION

There are many prayer needs as we step out to fulfill our destiny. Find a partner who would take one day to fast and pray for one common goal. For example, pray for a church who is in need of finances to build a community kitchen, pray for a family who is faced with a possible eviction, and there are many more needs. As you pray, write down in your journal or notepad, what the Master is speaking to you. He may give you directions on how to assist with these needs.

PRAYER OF REPENTANCE AND RESTORATION

Pray the following prayer if you feel you have missed your time or season to complete the Master's work.

Jesus, I am sorry that I have missed the time or opportunity You presented to me in the past. Please forgive me for putting other things before You and becoming distracted by the cares of life. If You will allow me once again to experience all that You have for me, I will use my gifts and talents for Your glory. Thank You, heavenly Father, for hearing me. In Jesus's name, amen.

Don't worry about your age or socioeconomic status. God still has a plan for you. He loves you and wants the very best for you. Lay hold of the truths in this book, and watch Him do amazing things in and through you!

THE CHARGE

I CHALLENGE YOU TO explore, discover, and embrace your gift of grace the Master has created you with. Move forward and accomplish all He has for you. Wherever you are on your journey with the King, continue until you fulfill your destiny. Yes, there may be some risks to step out of your comfort zone—a place where the rules of engagement are unfamiliar, oftentimes even hostile, and possibly limited, where jealousy and a spirit of competition flares up and even attempts to overtake you as you engage one at the frontline. Remember, the enemy, Satan, does not play by the rules, neither does he play fair.

You are the winner! Your steps have been ordered. You have been given your marching orders. You have been given permission to step into unlimited places of opportunities the Master has for you. He has made a promise "…to never leave you nor forsake you" (Heb. 13:5).

With your gift of grace, you will be a reformer, a change agent, in a new territory or region to pull down or destroy walls of traditions and to save many people. Propel forward and do not look back except to send a praise report of the marvelous things you have discovered and encountered as you fulfill your purpose in the kingdom of God.

SUGGESTED RESOURCES

Kenneth E. Hagin, Sr., *The Power Gifts of the Spirit: Gifts of Faith, Working of Miracles and Gifts of Healings* (Tulsa, OK: Kenneth Hagin Ministries, 2012).

Bill Hamon, *Ministering Spiritual Gifts* (Santa Rosa Beach, FL: Christian International Ministries Network, 2006).

Bill Hamon, *Prophets and Personal Prophesy, God's Prophetic Voice Today* (Shippensburg, PA: Destiny Image Publishers, 1987).

Kenneth Cain Kinghorn, *Gifts of the Spirit* (Nashville, TN: Abingdon Press, 1976). He also has a Spiritual Gifts Questionnaire Assessment booklet.

Kenneth Cain Kinghorn, *Discovering Your Spiritual Gifts, A Personal Inventory Method*, (Grand Rapids: MI: Zondervan, 1981).

C. Peter Wagner, *Discover Your Spiritual Gifts* (Bloomington, MN: Chosen Books, 2012).

C. Peter Wagner, *Your Spiritual Gifts Can Help Your Church Grow* (Ventura, CA: Regal Books, 1979).

David Walters, *The Gifts of the Spirits, A Children, and Adult Bible Study on the Gifts of the Spirit*, (Macon, GA: Good News Fellowship Ministries, 2005).

Ruth Vander Zee, *Youth Discover Your Gifts and How to Use Them* (Grand Rapids, MI: Faith Alive Christian Resources, 1998).

Spiritual gifts questionnaire—C. Peter Wagner's *Finding Your Spiritual Gifts Questionnaire: The Easy to Use, Self-Guided Questionnaire* can be purchased through online retailers such as Christianbook.com and Amazon.com. It is also included in his book *Discover Your Spiritual Gifts*, referenced previously.

NOTES

INTRODUCTION

1. Dictionary.com, s.v. "potential," http://www.dictionary
.com/browse/potential.

1—THE SECRET

1. Saul McCleod, "Erik Erickson, Simply Psychology,"
https://simplypsychology.org/Erik-Erikson.html.
2. Ibid.
3. Ibid.

2—DISCOVERING YOUR GIFTS OF GRACE

1. Merriam-Websters.com, s.v. "delight," https://www
.merriam-webster.com/dictionary/delight.
2. William J. McRae, *The Dynamics of Spiritual Gifts*,
(Grand Rapids, MI: Zondervan Publishing House, 1976),
22.
3. *Vine's Expository Dictionary of NT Words*, s.v. "*charis*,"
https://www.studylight.org/dictionaries/ved/g/gift-giving
.html.
4. BlueLetterBible.org, s.v. "ekklesia," https://www
.blueletterbible.org/lang/Lexicon/Lexicon.cfm?strongs
=G1577&t=KJV.
5. McRae, *The Dynamics of Spiritual Gifts*; C. Peter Wagner,
Discover Your Spiritual Gifts (Bloomington, MN: Chosen
Books, 2012).

3—ESTABLISHING AND ACTIVATING
YOUR GIFTS OF GRACE

1. Wikipedia.com, s.v. "Mother Teresa," https://en
   .wikipedia.org/wiki/Mother_Teresa.
2. Alvin J. Vander Griend, *Discover Your Gifts and Learn
   How to Use Them* (Grand Rapids, Michigan: Faith Alive
   Christian Resources, 1996), 22–23. Used by permission.

4—OVERCOMING THE FEAR OF RISK

1. Walter Dean Myers, *Slam* (New York City: Scholastic
   Paperbacks, 2008).
2. Merriam-Webster.com, s.v. "risk," https://www.merriam
   -webster.com/dictionary/risk.
3. Encarta Dictionary: English (North America), s.v.
   "combat," https://support.office.com/en-us/article/find
   -the-dictionary-to-look-up-words-79178811-b873-4c4b
   -aa4b-b7c8bc27dd73.
4. BlueLetterBible.org, s.v. "dumanis," https://www
   .blueletterbible.org/search/Dictionary/viewTopic.cfm
   ?topic=VT0000005, as quoted from *Vine's Expository
   Dictionary of New Testament Words Online.*
5. *Vine's New Testament Dictionary*, s.v. "*dumamis,*"https://
   www.studylight.org/dictionaries/ved/p/power.html.
6. The Henry Ford, "What If I Don't Move to the Back of
   the Bus?" https://www.thehenryford.org/explore/stories
   -of-innovation/what-if/rosa-parks/.
7. Samantha Page, "10 Maya Angelou Quotes That Will
   Inspire You to Do Better," *O, The Oprah Magazine*, May
   2014, http://www.oprahmag.co.za/oprah's-world/news/10
   -maya-angelou-quotes-that-will-inspire-you-to-do-better.

5—HIDDEN IN THE HOUSE

1. Dictionary.com, s.v. "hidden,"http://www.dictionary.com
   /browse/hidden?s=t.

2. Bill Hamon, *Ministering Spiritual Gifts* (Santa Rosa Beach, FL: Christian International Ministries Network, 2006), 4–12.

3. Dictionary.com, s.v. "unveiled," https//www.dictionary.com/browse/unveiled.

4. Dale A. Robbins, "How to Keep from Getting Hurt in a Church," Victorious.org, http://www.victorious.org/howhurt.htm. Used by permission.

5. John Bevere, *The Bait of Satan* (Lake Mary, FL: Charisma House, 1996), 8. Used by permission.

6. All the gifts of grace were not listed in chapter 3; just twenty. Worship is also a gift of grace. The biblical support may be found in 1 Samuel 16:23; 1 Chronicles 9:33; 2 Chronicles 5:12–14.

7. John Bevere, *The Bait of Satan* (Lake Mary, FL: Charisma House, 1996). Used by permission.

6—YOUR ANOINTING IS TOO COSTLY FOR YOU TO REMAIN QUIET

1. BlueLetterBible.org, s.v. *"chrio,"* https://www.blueletterbible.org/lang/Lexicon/Lexicon.cfm?strongs=G5548&t=KJV.

2. Timothy Stokes, *Handling the Anointing* (Flint, MI: Word of Life Publishing, 1994), 1–2. Used by permission.

3. Ibid.

4. Guillermo Maldonado, *How to Walk in the Supernatural Power of God* (New Kensington, PA: Whitaker House, 2011), 126. Used by permission.

7—YOUR SEAT OF DESTINY

1. Cambridge Academic Dictionary Online, s.v. "destine."

2. Leonardo DaVinci, www.totalhistory.com/mona-lisa.

3. GotQuestions.org, "What Is the Significance of a City Gate in the Bible?" https://www.gotquestions.org/city-gate.html.

4. Bible.gen.nz, s.v. "gate," https://bible.gen.nz/amos/archaeology/gate.htm.
5. Cambridge Academic Dictionary Online, s.v., "shift."
6. Cambridge Academic Dictionary Online, s.v., "unveil."

PART II—BUILDING YOUR SPIRITUAL TOOLBOX

1. I have attempted to research online and other resources to find if this story belongs to another author. I have searched to no avail. If you know the author of this story, please contact me at the address on the copyright page and I will promptly request permission to use this story.

8—THE KEY OF WISDOM

1. Encarta English Dictionary Online, s.v. "wisdom," https://support.office.com/en-us/article/find-the-dictionary-to-look-up-words-79178811-b873-4c4b-aa4b-b7c8bc27dd73.
2. "What Is Wisdom?," Gathering Wisdom, http://www.gatheringwisdom.com/gwchap1.html; see also Jerry Fletcher, Cheryl Matschek, Al Siebert, and Gail Tycer, *Gathering Wisdom* (Portland, OR: Practical Psychology Press, 2003). Used by permission.
3. Gloria Copeland, *And Jesus Healed Them All* (Fort Worth, TX: Kenneth Copeland Publications, 1981), 25–26.
4. Fletcher, Matschek, Siebert, and Tycer, *GatheringWisdom*, http://www.gatheringwisdom.com/gwchap1.html.

9—THE KEY OF PRAYER

1. Bartleby.com, "Abraham Lincoln," http://www.bartleby.com/348/authors/328.html.
2. Oswald Chambers, *Prayer: A Holy Occupation* (Grand Rapids, MI: Discovery House Publishers, 1992). Used by permission.
3. As quoted in Karen Moore, *Bible Promises for the Graduate* (Nashville, TN: B&H Publishing Group, 2014), 86.

4. Blueletterbible.org, s.v. "*pater*," https://www
.blueletterbible.org/lang/Lexicon/Lexicon.cfm?strongs
=G3962&t=KJV.

5. Søren Kierkegaard quote found at http://www
.sorenkierkegaard.nl/.

10—THE KEY OF FAITH

1. TheFamousPeople.com, s.v. "Ben Carson," https://www
.thefamouspeople.com/profiles/ben-carson-5393.php.

2. Ibid.

3. "77 Thought-Provoking Quotes by Ben Carson,"https://
quotes.thefamouspeople.com/ben-carson-5393.php; Ben
Carson and Cecil Murphey, *Gifted Hands* (Grand Rapids,
MI: Zondervan, 2011), 239.

4. TheFamousPeople.com, s.v. "Ben Carson."

5. W.E. Vine, *Reflections on Words of the New Testament*
(Nashville, TN: Thomas Nelson, 2011), 53.

6. Judy Kuriansky, PhD, "Martin Luther King Jr. Words of
Wisdom: Apply to Your Life," *Huffington Post*, March 22,
2014, https://www.huffingtonpost.com/judy-kuriansky
-phd/martin-luther-king-jr-wor_b_4624747.html.

7. BlueLetterBible.org, s.v. "phobos," https://www
.blueletterbible.org/lang/Lexicon/Lexicon.cfm?strongs
=G5401&t=KJV.

8. "BeliefNet's Inspirational Quotes: Ralph Waldo Emerson,"
http://www.beliefnet.com/quotes/inspiration/r/ralph
-waldo-emerson/all-i-have-seen-teaches-me-to-trust-the
-creator-fo.aspx.

9. Cambridge Academic Dictionary Online. s.v. "model."

10. Ibid., s.v. "imitation."

11. Goodreads.com, "Max Lucado Quotes,"https://www
.goodreads.com/quotes/14109-faith-is-not-the-belief-that
-god-will-do-what.

12. BrainyQuote.com, Corrie Ten Boom Quotes, https://www
.brainyquote.com/quotes/corrie_ten_boom_381184.

11—THE KEY OF GOD'S WORD—YOUR COMPASS

1. Merriam-Webster's Dictionary, s.v. "compass," https://www.merriam-webster.com/dictionary/compass.
2. W. Scott Lamb, "W. Scott Lamb: Theodore Roosevelt's Famous Quote About College," *The Washington Times*, July 28, 2015, https://www.washingtontimes.com/news/2015/jul/28/w-scott-lamb-theodore-roosevelts-famous-quote-about/.

12—THE KEY OF ACCOUNTABILITY

1. Dictionary.com, s.v. "accountable," http://www.dictionary.com/browse/accountable.
2. Joe Willmore, *No Magic Bullet* (Alexandria, VA: ASTD Press, 2009), 45. Used by permission.
3. Encarta English Dictionary, s.v. "commit," https://support.office.com/en-us/article/find-the-dictionary-to-look-up-words-79178811-b873-4c4b-aa4b-b7c8bc27dd73.
4. Encarta English Dictionary, s.v. "coagulation formation of a mass of blood," https://support.office.com/en-us/article/find-the-dictionary-to-look-up-words-79178811-b873-4c4b-aa4b-b7c8bc27dd73.
5. Dictionary.com, s.v. "mentor," http://www.dictionary.com/browse/mentor?s=t.

13—THE KEY OF PREPARATION

1. Zig Ziglar, "You Were Born to Win," Ziglar.com, August 22, 2015, https://www.ziglar.com/quotes/you-were-born-to-win-but-to-be-a-winner/.
2. English Oxford Living Dictionaries, s.v. "preparation," https://en.oxforddictionaries.com/definition/us/preparation.
3. Merriam-Webster.com, s.v. "prepare," https://www.merriam-webster.com/dictionary/prepare.
4. Biography.com, s.v. "Lee Iacocca Biography," https://www.biography.com/people/lee-iacocca-9348614.

5. "Motivational and Inspirational Quotes About Preparation," http://www.motivational-inspirational-corner.com/getquote.html?categoryid=67.
6. "Believe in Yourself, Have Faith in Your Abilities," http://motivationalreads.com/believe-faith-abilities/.

14—THE KEY OF TIMING

1. BlueLetterBible.org, s.v. "*chronos*," https://www.blueletterbible.org/lang/lexicon/lexicon.cfm?t=kjv&strongs=g5550.
2. Tracy V. Wilson, "How Fast Food Works," HowStuffWorks, https://science.howstuffworks.com/innovation/edible-innovations/fast-food3.htm.
3. BlueLetterBible.org, s.v. "*kairos*," https://www.blueletterbible.org/lang/lexicon/lexicon.cfm?strongs=G2540; see also McKinley Valentine, "Chronos and Kairos,"https://mckinleyvalentine.com/kairos/.
4. Roberts Liardon, *Spiritual Timing* (Tulsa, OK: Albury Publishing, 1996), 47–48. The author, through his secretary, gave me permission to use this text in my book. I attempted to locate and contact the publisher to obtain permission. I had no success due to limited information from publisher, which only indicated this book was out of date and they no longer published it. Therefore, I called the author directly. His secretary informed me that author currently self-publishes all his books.
5. Ibid., 49.
6. BlueLetterBible.org, s.v. "*exagorazo*," https://www.blueletterbible.org/lang/lexicon/lexicon.cfm?t=kjv&strongs=g1805.

ABOUT THE AUTHOR

Doris E. Golder is the president of D'vine Strategies LLC. She is a visionary strategist who trains, equips, and motivates individuals to discover, be released, and walk in their purpose. She is an advocate for those who feel they have no voice. She has conducted workshops for Youth Development and Gifts of Grace. The author has a heart for the heavy mandate pastors carry in this End Time. At times, she will extend an invitation to walk with them as a spiritual coach. She uses the key of wisdom and provides encouragement to shepherds as they equip the sheep to identify their spiritual gifts (gifts of grace) and walk in them.

Doris is the former founder and servant leader for Travailing Ministries International Inc. (TMII), a nonprofit organization from 2009–2018. The organization held workshops on spiritual development, assisted youth with book scholarships, and provided community and humanitarian resources. Doris utilizes prayer as her platform recognizing that faith and prayer are the power sources that please and move the hand of God.

An ordained minister and chaplain, Doris earned a bachelor of art degree in business management, a master's degree in urban ministry with a concentration in marriage and family. She is a K–12 school counselor.

CONTACT INFORMATION

www.dvinestrategies.com
doris@dvinestrategies.com

CPSIA information can be obtained
at www.ICGtesting.com
Printed in the USA
LVHW050153080221
678682LV00012B/772

9 781733 853408